"*No Weigh!* will guide you to realize that 'happy is the new hot,' and how to snuff out thoughts about a negative body image and debunk myths about diets. Every teen needs this book right now!"

—*Louann Brizendine, M.D., author of*
The Female Brain *and* The Male Brain

"The journey through adolescence is made a bit easier in the hands of this trio of experts who share their wisdom about food, sleep, weight, texting, exercise, emotions, and more. Teens (and their parents) are skillfully guided through this potential minefield by science-based, compassionate advice and with gentle humor laid out in short, easy-to-read chapters—with plenty of questions to invite reflection and space for teens to journal their responses."

—*Karen R. Koenig, author of seven books on eating and weight, including* Helping Patients Outsmart Overeating

"*No Weigh!* is a must-read for teens! This easy-to-read, informative book is sure to change lives."

—*Jenni Schaefer, author of* Life Without Ed,
Goodbye Ed, Hello Me, *and* Almost Anorexic

"*No Weigh!* is a must-read for teens dealing with body-image and self-esteem issues. This engaging and readable book boils down the science on how to really develop a healthy sense of self."

—*Kristina Saffran, Co-Founder and
Chief Executive Officer of Project HEAL*

"Practical, fun, funny, and incredibly useful. Want to embrace your life and yourself? Dip in anywhere, and you'll get stuff you need—and want—to use. IMHO, there's no way to live without *No Weigh!*"

—*Joe Kelly, Co-Founder, New Moon Girls and
author of* Dads and Daughters

"*No Weigh!* is the resource I've wished for as a psychologist and eating disorder specialist for years! It is an accessible, easy-to-understand read for teens and parents. I highly recommend this book to anyone who wants an affirming read for compassionately connecting with your body through the teen years."

—*Janean Anderson, Ph.D., CEDS, Licensed Psychologist,
Certified Eating Disorders Specialist, author of* Recover Your
Recovery Podcast

of related interest

My Anxiety Handbook
Getting Back on Track
Sue Knowles, Bridie Gallagher and Phoebe McEwen
Illustrated by Emmeline Pidgen
ISBN 978 1 78592 440 8
eISBN 978 1 78450 813 5

The Healthy Coping Colouring Book and Journal
Creative Activities to Help Manage Stress, Anxiety and Other Big Feelings
Pooky Knightsmith
Illustrated by Emily Hamilton
ISBN 978 1 78592 139 1
eISBN 978 1 78450 405 2

Banish Your Body Image Thief
A Cognitive Behavioural Therapy Workbook on Building
Positive Body Image for Young People
Kate Collins-Donnelly
ISBN 978 1 84905 463 8
eISBN 978 0 85700 842 8

NO WEIGH!

A Teen's Guide to Positive Body Image, Food, and Emotional Wisdom

SIGNE DARPINIAN, WENDY STERLING,
AND SHELLEY AGGARWAL

Foreword by Connie Sobczak

Jessica Kingsley *Publishers*
London and Philadelphia

First published in 2018
by Jessica Kingsley Publishers
73 Collier Street
London N1 9BE, UK
and
400 Market Street, Suite 400
Philadelphia, PA 19106, USA

www.jkp.com

Library of Congress Cataloging in Publication Data
A CIP catalog record for this book is available from the Library of Congress

British Library Cataloguing in Publication Data
A CIP catalogue record for this book is available from the British Library

ISBN 978 1 78592 825 3
eISBN 978 1 78450 946 0

Printed and bound in Great Britain

MIX
Paper from
responsible sources
FSC
www.fsc.org   FSC® C013056

Contents

Foreword by Connie Sobczak   7

Acknowledgments 13

Introduction 15

PART I: THE BUILDING BLOCKS

1. On Your Mark, Get Set—Adolescence!. 21
2. Emotions 35
3. Learning Our Stress System. 45
4. Get Your ZZZZZZs! 57
5. Exercise 69

PART II: THE ESSENTIALS FOR CONNECTED EATING

6. Making Foods Equal in Availability 87
7. The Hunger Meter: Learning our Body's Language . . 97
8. Eating with Manageable Hunger 105
9. All Foods Are Fair Game. 115
10. Stopping at Just Enough. 131

PART III: ADDING TOOLS TO YOUR TOOLBOX

11. What to Do When You Want Food,
But You're Not Hungry 143
12. Food and Body Image for Special Events. 159
13. The More Often You Weigh, the More You'll Weigh . 171

Conclusion 185

Resources 187

References 191

Foreword

I often wonder how my life would have been different if I had read a book like this when I was a teenager. I didn't like my body at all, and I treated it terribly. I thought it was the cause of all of my problems. I thought that if I could just perfect my body (code for lose weight) like all of my friends were trying to do, my life would be perfect.

My body hatred began when I was in the eighth grade. At school, my friends were all starting to restrict their food and talk about their bodies in negative ways. At home, my dad was on my sister Stephanie's case about her weight. She was almost six-feet tall, wore size 12 shoes, and was just an all-around big person. I realize now that she was also binge eating due to the shame she felt about being so different from her friends. At the dinner table, my dad talked about the food she was eating, always telling her how many calories were in everything, and suggesting that she not eat so much.

After several months of my dad's comments, Stephanie decided to go to Weight Watchers. She lost weight, but, like 95 percent of dieters who go to programs like Weight Watchers do (that's 95 out of 100 people!), she gained the weight back, plus more. At this point she was very unhappy with her body, which led to the development of bulimia.

Being surrounded by so much body hatred and dieting at home and school led me straight into my own eating disorder.

From the age of 15 to almost 22, I struggled with bulimia. I lost out on so much fun I could have had in my teen years and early adulthood, just because I thought my thighs and butt were too big! Granted, my "friends" in middle school and high school used to tease me by calling me "thunder thighs" and "bubble butt" and other not-so-nice names, so it's not surprising I wanted to change my body. But the cost was really high. And even when I was at my thinnest, my life was no better than it had been before.

I had my eating disorder at a time when there wasn't a lot of support, let alone awareness, so I had to find my own way out of my suffering. I finally realized that my body hatred was disrupting all of the wonderful plans I had for my future, and that it was making it really hard to stay in school. I left college for a while to heal myself. Lots of positive changes happened at that point, and I made it to a place of appreciation for my body and a balanced relationship with food and exercise. Fortunately, I got back to school and finished my degree, but my body hatred nearly blocked me from doing so.

My sister Stephanie wasn't so lucky. She never got over her eating disorder, and she also was poisoned by the silicone that leaked through her blood stream from a faulty breast implant. She died at the age of 36, leaving behind two young children and a grieving family.

That was the moment when I realized I had to change the world. My daughter Carmen was a year old when her aunt Stephanie died, and I wanted to make sure that she—and all children—would know that their bodies were something to enjoy and celebrate, all the way through the changes of the teen years and beyond. I didn't want Carmen to suffer like Stephanie and I had, and I didn't want anyone else to either.

Fast forward to now, and the nonprofit I created, The Body Positive, has made it possible for thousands of people to value their unique identities and become free from self-hatred so they can use their energy and intellect to make positive changes in their own lives, communities, and beyond.

I tell you my story with the goal that you'll see why developing a peaceful relationship with your body and learning how to practice connected eating and balanced exercise are so important. I want you to know, like my daughter and other teens who grew up with The Body Positive know, that your body is exactly as it is meant to be, so there is no need to waste any of your precious time listening to messages that tell you otherwise.

It's important to remember that a whole lot of people gave you the body you have. Think about all of your ancestors that go back to the very first human. Every single one of them had the "perfect" body—because they lived! Each one thrived, connected with another human to create the next generation, and on and on until you were born. Even if you don't know any of your ancestors because you're adopted, it doesn't matter because they still existed and managed to get you here, and you can imagine who they were. When we realize that our bodies carry the lives of a whole lot of amazing people in them, it's harder to trash them and treat them poorly.

I'm excited for you to dive into *No Weigh!*, so you can learn more about your body and how to have the most enjoyment with it. I have to say I think you lucked out. You're in great hands with Signe, Wendy, and Shelley!

This book is filled with fun activities (I love the worksheets!) that give tools for having a great relationship to food and finding balance with exercise unrelated to your weight. *No Weigh!* also covers other important topics, like tips for how to get enough sleep and why that is so important for your life, and useful information about emotions and how to deal with them. You'll learn some really cool science that shows why caring for your body with kindness makes so much sense, and why focusing on your weight instead of on how you treat your body will lead to some pretty bad outcomes. Everything you'll read will move you towards having more fun in your life because you won't be wasting time being preoccupied about the truly amazing body you inhabit.

The most important thing to remember as you read this book is that you deserve respect and love—just as you are in this moment, even with your changing body and what you think of as your "flaws." Maybe you don't see this now, but life is short, no matter how long we live, and we're supposed to enjoy it. What I found for myself was that being critical of my body did nothing to make my life better. So why not dive in now, and learn how to create the most positive relationship with yourself that you can?

I'm not saying every day will be a barrel of laughs, even after doing the important work of connecting with your body. If you think of your relationships with other people, like your family or friends, you know that some days are great, and others aren't so fun. If you can be with your body in this same way, it takes a lot of pressure off because you know that you're going to have some tough days—that's life—but it doesn't mean that your overall relationship with yourself is a bad one. In the tough moments, you just need to focus more attention on the friendship you have with your body. It's like with your friends, if you get in a fight it helps to talk things out, so you can get back to having fun.

I'm guessing that you've gotten a lot of messages, like I did, that make you feel that your real "job" right now is to do anything you can to "perfect" your body. It's important to remember when you feel this way that lots of corporations and individuals are making tons of money off your body dissatisfaction and your attempts to "fix" it. They create messages to make you feel this way, so they can get you to spend your money on their products and services.

The teen years are supposed to be about rebelling, so why not be a rebel by learning to love your body and treat it well? This is a radical thing to do in this world where most people you know probably dislike their bodies. Reading *No Weigh!* is a perfect place to start your own revolution.

I invite you to join the growing Body Positive movement, where people who are diverse in every way you can think of are doing the work to grow in self-love and create a peaceful relationship with their bodies. I'll leave you with the wise words of one of our teen Body Positive leaders: "It's all how you feel about your own body, because *this is home*. And if you're not comfortable at home, you're not going to be comfortable anywhere else. *The revolution starts with you!*"

Connie Sobczak, author of *Embody: Learning to Love Your Unique Body (and quiet that critical voice!)* and Co-Founder of The Body Positive
May 29, 2018

Acknowledgments

We would like to acknowledge those who have assisted us in the growth of this project: Riley Nickols, Ph.D., counseling and sport psychologist, for contributing his wisdom in our exercise chapter; Margaret R. Hunter, art therapist and author of *Reflections of Body Image in Art Therapy*, for her contribution of her art therapy techniques; Rick Hanson, Ph.D., for generously lending his time to dialogue about experiential methods to introduce *taking in the good* to teens; Louann Brizendine, M.D., for a lively interview about the teen brain; Dr. B. Timothy Walsh, professor of psychiatry at Columbia University, for his assistance in infusing the habit-based model excerpts; Mark Warren, M.D., chief medical officer at The Emily Program, for his expertise on males and eating disorders; Drew Logue, M.D., for lending his time, ideas, and for helping us shape our sleep chapter; Anita Johnston, Ph.D., for her generosity in allowing us to use her body awareness exercises; Lucy Aphramor, Ph.D., R.D., for graciously lending the "Why We Eat What We Eat" activity from her Well Now approach; and Joe Kelly, who added his organization, edits and references. And last but not least, we would like to thank Jessica Kingsley Publishers for their willingness to take on this project to support teens around their body image, food, and emotions. Many of you have been our teachers; your work has informed our work and we are so grateful.

We would be remiss if we didn't mention those who personally supported and encouraged us from idea to publication.

Signe would like to thank her mother, Sonja Knutsen, for her unconditional love from concept to finished product. Her mother never said one bad thing about her body or her eating growing up, making it easy to pass along body positivity. She'd like to thank her daughter, Andie Darpinian, the love of her life, for understanding what her job is about, and for knowing that "loving your body is a really good thing." Signe would also like to thank Dr. Brenda Schaeffer for her ongoing wisdom and mentoring, and Holly M. Davies for her spot-on guidance and support through the whole process.

Wendy would like to thank her mentors and colleagues who have helped shape her way of thinking about food and weight. She would like to thank her parents Fran and Stuart Meyer and her sister Bonnie Altman for their unconditional love and support, and for creating a diet-free household where all foods were allowed. She thanks daughters Emily and Lexi Sterling for their dance shows, songs, and letters, and for being her best partners in the kitchen, experimenting with new foods and recipes. Lastly, she would also like to thank her husband Peter Sterling, for his endless patience, gentle heart, friendship, and love.

Shelley Aggarwal would like to thank her mother and father, Ramey and Vijay Aggarwal, for all that they have given her, and all that they have taught her. She would also like to thank her husband Ravi as well as the teachers, mentors, and loved ones who have supported and guided her.

Introduction

We would like to welcome all of you who have decided to take the journey with us through this book. If you have picked up this book on your own, give yourself an internal high-five for making your well-being a priority. If someone who cares about you has handed you this book, we applaud them for supporting you in exploring and questioning what it means to be truly well, in relation to your food, body image, and the experiences and emotions that surround these topics. The reality is that these issues don't have to be super serious, and through *No Weigh! A Teen's Guide to Positive Body Image, Food, and Emotional Wisdom*, we are hoping to give you the scoop on what's happening during the teen years so that life can be less confusing and even good during this dynamic time.

Maybe you're someone who is very well informed? For you, we think this book will add to your knowledge about how bodies change, emotionally and physically, in the teen years, and why nutrition is not only important but critical for growth and development. For the rest of you, who try to stay well informed, but suddenly discover how completely fascinating the wall color is in your bedroom the night before a test, we know this book's going to add to your knowledge (and no doubt your walls are pretty cool).

The message in this book is simple, we want you to have a friendship with food. It's a lifelong relationship, so why not make it a great one? We eat often during the day, so why not eat with pleasure, joy, and happiness? It might sound corny, but sometimes corny is exactly what we need.

You've probably been told to "work hard," to "study hard," to make "healthy choices" and "good choices," and "to do the right thing." *But*, how often have you been told to work and study and make decisions with joy and happiness? We know that people your age have tons of pressure on them on a daily basis. These pressures over time can lead to neglecting yourself in an effort to meet the demands of the life around you by "working hard" and "studying hard," etc. This book and the knowledge in it is to help make life a little easier and to add to your joy by empowering you with knowledge.

We wrote the workbook as "bite size," given you're probably strapped for time and you have to get back to that incredible wall color anyway. We know you don't have time to read a lengthy book in the midst of high school academics, sports, and a social life. The content can be read quickly and the exercises can be completed as time permits. By using techniques such as journaling, which has been scientifically shown to calm emotional reactivity, and offering information about why certain things happen the way they do in the teen years, we hope to make navigating this sometimes stressful time of life a bit easier. The skills and tools in this book are meant to stay with you as you enter various stages of life such as college or work and beyond. Walls at work can be even more fascinating when you have a deadline coming up. Just sayin'.

A problem requires a solution that's matched to it. Each chapter will provide you with skills meant to be a working entity, meaning they are not meant to be used once, but over and over again. If you keep practicing, you will get really good at pairing the challenge you are dealing with with the appropriate skill set, whether that challenge be related to stress, body image concerns, emotional ups and downs, sleep, or connected eating. We have designed these exercises based on our combined experiences and expertise. Most of the exercises are preceded by a client sample or a sample we have come up with to help you gain insight or to give you suggestions for how to go about them. The exercises can be done on your own or with help from parents, or with professional guidance. Feel free to pick and choose among the exercises. You can use them as "prompts," they may speak to you as they are, or maybe they ignite an idea of your own; either way, be sure to adapt our suggestions to fit your own needs.

In Part I of this book we will give you an overview of foundational items like puberty, emotions, stress, sleep, and exercise. Part II focuses on the essentials for connected eating: eating to appetite, eating what appeals to you, and stopping at just enough. Part III is about adding tools to your toolbox.

No Weigh! A Teen's Guide to Positive Body Image, Food, and Emotional Wisdom is meant for a diverse readership, but has been written specifically for those of you who are in the beginning and middle of the teen years. However, the concepts are universal and the information here is relevant for us all. And by "us," we truly mean us all. We are writing this book for teens who are cis-gender (male or female), gender-fluid, transgender and all other wonderful ways of being.

Last but not least, this book has three authors. Therefore, we use "we" most of the time because it represents our combined voice. When we need to specify one author over the other, we use the author's name: Signe, Shelley, or Wendy.

So, fasten your seatbelts, we look forward to sharing this road trip with you toward your overall well-being!

A Note to the Reader

Most of us come into the world knowing how to eat in response to our self-regulatory system. There are exceptions, however, for people who have medical conditions. Our book will outline how to become a fearless eater and to eat according to your own hunger and satiety cues. However, some of what we will be talking about may not be possible for people who have to follow strict dietary guidelines due to a medical issue, food allergies, or an intolerance. For them, there is a real need to avoid certain types of food or else they will get sick, feel bad, or have an allergic reaction.

Allergies and intolerances have increased. We see trends of people avoiding gluten, dairy, sugar, etc. Some decide to change how they are eating because their friend is doing it, or their Aunt Sally is doing it. Others may hide behind an intolerance/allergy as a way to avoid having to eat something. We ask readers who are avoiding something to be honest with themselves. Has a medical doctor told you that you need to follow a certain diet? Do you have a medical diagnosis that necessitates eating a certain way? Does avoiding certain foods improve a physical condition you have? If you answered yes to any of these questions, then some aspects of this book will not apply to you. Or, is there a chance that you are avoiding a food group to lose weight or change your body in a certain way? If your dietary avoidance is not medically necessary, we ask readers to be open to the idea of adding it back in. This may feel scary, but, ultimately, the goal is to be a fearless eater—someone who can eat anything and feel comfortable in their own body.

Part I

The Building Blocks

Chapter 1

On Your Mark, Get Set—Adolescence!

The teenage years...what's going on? Is the world deliberately trying to confuse us? We're sitting around minding our own business and suddenly our bodies go berserk. Puberty is a lot like your smartphone; the minute you start to understand all of your new apps, it's already time for an update again.

It's kinda cool to know about the changes that come along with puberty before they happen, and to remind yourself that everybody goes through it. No two people are alike, but one thing adults have in common is that they made it through puberty, and so will you.

Puberty is that time in life during which humans; males, females, gender-fluid individuals, go through a growth process in which their body changes from being a kid body to an adult body. This process usually takes a few years. Different people enter puberty at different times, and progress through it at different rates. This is why two 13-year-old people can be in totally different stages of development, and look completely different. Some people start puberty as early as 8 or 9 years old (although this is on the younger end of the spectrum) and others may not start until 14 years old (that's on the older end of the same spectrum). All of these people are "normal." Normal is in quotes because there is no absolute normal. There are ranges, like starting puberty between 8 and 14 years old, and as you can see, "normal" can be the difference of 5–6 years. We are all unique and that is the most "normal" truth about us all.

As mentioned above, puberty involves change and is the time when we start growing into our adult bodies and progressing through important growth milestones. Girls can anticipate starting their periods, developing breasts, and noting hair growth in their armpits and genital area. Boys will have some of the same changes, with hair growth in their armpits and genital areas. They will also notice a deepening voice (sometimes starting with a deep bass sound, finishing with a sound of a frazzled harmonica, in the span of a single sentence) and development of their genitalia. Most adolescents get acne, i.e. pimples. Everyone is so busy being freaked out about their own pimples, they won't have the time to worry about yours (thank you, puberty, you're like a spiritual practice). You also get taller and the body develops more into an adult shape. Think about how different a 10-year-old's body is from that of a 19-year-old.

Some people can have abnormal pubertal development. Some people may start puberty early, before age 8 or 9, and others may note that they have not had any signs of pubertal changes as they are getting older. If you have concerns, talk to your doctor and ask questions. Don't avoid the conversation, as puberty is a natural part of development and it's okay to talk about it. Sometimes progressing through puberty too early or too late can be due to medical reasons, so having the conversation with your doctor could really give you insight into what's going on with your own body.

The Shape of Things to Come

What color are your eyes? How about your hair? How tall are you? Do these things seem similar to your parents? Are you similar to an uncle, maybe a cousin or even your sister or brother? Or maybe you don't know your biological family at all? You might look totally different from all of them, whether you know them or not. Have you ever considered how you became you?

The human body is pretty awesome. The science of who we are can lead us to understand why we are so similar to our relatives and also how we can be so different from them as well. Some of who we are is pre-programmed. Genes (not jeans, but those are cute too) are the instruction manual for the body. We are born with this manual that is made from our parents' manual, that is made from their parents', that is made from their parents', and so on and so on. So, do you see how we can be a lot like our parents because their manual is the closest copy to ours, and how we can also be very different because pieces of our instructions can go back generations and generations? Sometimes parts of the instructions that are downloaded for you could be the ones from your great-great-great-grandparents. This is the reason that sometimes we could look much more like a relative in an old family photo and not the brother or sister we are standing next to.

Our bodies are designed so that we have features or characteristics similar to our families, but the amazing thing is that we are all unique as well. Change happens even within your genes. Our instruction manual is influenced by our life, the environment that we live in and our choices. Some of these influences could be where we live, the food that we eat, exercise, and even stress. These and other influences can sometimes change parts of our instruction manual. It's a little like we write in some extra information or we sometimes delete parts of the manual or mix some of the sentences around. This really interesting field of biology is called epigenetics and it explores how our environment changes the way our instruction manual is expressed. We could write a whole book on this topic alone. Some change is designed by your genes and some change is not planned, and is determined by the experiences and choices we make.

Part of who you are is related to the manual you came with, such as your height. Your height is mainly determined by your family's genes. Your height will closely resemble your biological mom and dad's height. In general, girls end up near their biological mom's height and boys end up near their biological dad's height. This may not always be the case but it's true most of the time.

During your teen years you will get most of your adult height. What does that mean? It means that boys and girls have a growth spurt during puberty. Adequate nutrition is the fundamental building block for healthy development. Like a plant which requires sunlight, air, soil, and water to grow, our bodies need vitamins, minerals, fats, carbohydrates, proteins, and many other things to grow. The primary way we obtain these essential components is through a variety of foods and fluids.

It is also important that a person is eating enough food. Eating too little can interrupt the growth and development process that is linked to your manual. The key is to eat in a way that supports this time of growth while keeping in mind that all fare is fair and each food has its own superhero powers.

One common misunderstanding in our culture is that weight gain is somehow abnormal. Gaining weight is necessary in order for your body to be healthy. Just like your bones need to grow in length as well as become stronger to be the support system for your body, your organs, including your brain, are growing and changing. Did you know that 60 percent of your brain is adipose tissue? "Adipose" is fancy for fat. Your brain tissue is almost all fat. It's trendy for the culture to promote an anti-fat message, but we actually need fat on our body. Fat, or adipose tissue, helps to protect our organs and keep them safe. Fat helps to keep us warm, and helps us to keep our hormones functioning normally.

Girls and boys distribute adipose tissue in their bodies differently. Girls can have more adipose in their arms and around their thighs, hips, and abdomens. This is one of the reasons that the bodies of boys and girls start to look different as we go through puberty. Girls develop more rounded hips and waists. However, our culture creates false values about certain shapes and sizes and some people feel unhappy because they think that they should look a certain way. You would never say, "I've gotta lose some height," or "I've gotta gain some height." Consider the same with your weight, the idea here is your natural weight. One of our goals in this book is to help you understand that we are unique and that our bodies are different and unique, as they should be.

Some of us will naturally be at higher weights, some of us at lower weights, and some of us will hang out somewhere in the middle. By understanding that change is normal, we hope you can find greater acceptance of your body, and the idea that normal is as varied as each one of us on this planet.

The Gifts I Have to Share Besides My Cool Hair

We want you to feel empowered with who you are by recognizing the gifts and strengths you bring to the table. By building your positivity muscles through appreciation for your own unique qualities (from the inside out), we are confident that this will help you feel more resilient. This first exercise is an opportunity for you to do this by listing 10 things that you like about yourself. Here's a client sample of how Cassidy tackled this task.

1. I'm curious.

2. I'm artistic.

3. I'm a good listener.

4. I'm chill.

5. I'm a good friend.

6. I see the goodness in others.

7. I appreciate my curves.

8. I think I have a pretty smile.

9. I've been told my eyes are sparkly.

10. I'm a good dancer, especially at weddings.

    It's so funny because, immediately after saying something positive, I wanted to write a list of all of the things I'm deficient at. A lot of these positives have a negative side to them as well, but focusing so much on the negative hides the strengths I also have.

We hope this example has given you some ideas for how to create your own list of 10 things that you like about yourself. On the next page you'll find a space for you to do this. If you still get stuck, ask your friends and family for ideas. Adjusting to the knowledge of who you are can take practice. Anytime you feel inadequate, come back to this exercise; building muscles happens through repetition.

THE GIFTS I HAVE TO SHARE
BESIDES MY COOL HAIR

1. _____
   _____

2. _____
   _____

3. _____
   _____

4. _____
   _____

5. _____
   _____

6. _____
   _____

7. _____
   _____

8. _____
   _____

9. _____
   _____

10. _____
    _____

Write On!

We are now going to do an exercise based on the principle of freewriting. Try to forget everything you've been told about writing for a moment. Freewriting is a style of writing where you set a timer, for, say, 3 minutes, and write non-stop during the time allotted for the exercise. The idea is to vent everything that is on your mind so that you clear it, leaving room for better feelings and thoughts. It's not healthy to keep your frustrations pent up inside, nor is it healthy to regurgitate them over and over again. After your timer goes off, make a commitment to stop hamster-wheeling, that repetitive rehashing of things in your mind, about your worries. Here's a client sample to show you how one teen approached this freewriting exercise. We hope it gives you an idea of the sorts of things you might like to write.

> I'm 13 years old and seem to be entering puberty later than my friends. I mean like I notice hair in places that I previously didn't have any, but all of their voices are changing and they are growing way taller than me. I'm not really that freaked out. I kinda like the idea of focusing on my head of hair because I think my hair is pretty cool, and because it's the one thing I can change about my appearance. I worry a little bit about girls not thinking I look good at pool parties, but I seem to get feedback that they don't really seem to notice that kind of stuff. They tell me I'm funny, that my humor is totally "out there," in a good way. I should just chill.

Now it's your turn to have a go at freewriting. Set your timer for 3 minutes and see what comes out. Don't worry about spelling or punctuation, just get to writing!

WRITE ON!

_____

_____

_____

_____

_____

_____

_____

_____

_____

_____

_____

_____

_____

_____

_____

_____

_____

_____

_____

_____

_____

_____

_____

_____

_____

_____

_____

_____

_____

Always a Dialogue Never a Monologue

Anita Johnston, author of *Eating in the Light of the Moon*, uses a technique when a negative body image thought or comparison pops up for her. The minute she finds herself stuck in a monologue (a prolonged talk or discourse by a single speaker, in this case, herself) about self-image, she commits to a dialogue (conversation between you and yourself, in this case).[1] See our own examples below:

> *Monologue*: "When is my voice going to get deeper like all my friends?"
> *Dialogue*: "Pubertal changes happen at different times for everyone, there is no 'right' time for my voice to change."
>
> *Monologue*: "I wish I was as thin as my friends."
> *Dialogue*: "Who says that they have the right bodies and I have the wrong one? We all have our own unique beauty, from the inside out."
>
> *Monologue*: "Girls only like tall guys and so far, I'm not growing..."
> *Dialogue*: "This thought is not in my best interest, so I'm going to let this thought go."

On the next page after "Monologue" write down a negative you tell yourself, and after "Dialogue" add a positive response to counter it. There's space for you to choose three different examples.

ALWAYS A DIALOGUE NEVER A MONOLOGUE

monologue: _____
_____
_____
_____

Dialogue: _____
_____
_____
_____

monologue: _____
_____
_____
_____

Dialogue: _____
_____
_____
_____

monologue: _____
_____
_____
_____

Dialogue: _____
_____
_____
_____

Affirmations Rule

Positive thinking helps effect change. The thoughts you have shape the action you take. Affirmations are specific positive thoughts you create in response to a current need or goal. Some people resist affirmations because they say they feel fake. The good news is that, in recent years, "fake it till you make it" (also called "act as if") has plenty of science to prove that you can fool yourself into a happier state.[2] Affirmations work best when your current emotional state is in a fairly good place to begin with. They are not suggested if mood is too low, given it may be difficult to self-generate positive thoughts and sustain them. You can use them to boost body image thoughts (or anything else for that matter), and if that's too hard, try borrowing the energy of someone else who you know feels confident in their body. Think Will Ferrell running naked through the city of Montrose in *Old School*. Here's an example:

1. I will have patience with the process of my changing body.

2. My body is my home in this lifetime.[3]

3. I have everything I need to handle this bad body image thought.

4. I am worthy of love and belonging, regardless of my weight and shape.

5. I trust my body's wisdom.

6. I am grateful for all my body does for me.

7. I am comfortable in my own skin.

8. Anyone would be lucky to be my friend.

9. I attract people who like me exactly how I am.

10. I love my body as it is today.

We hope you have found inspiration in the list above. Now it's time for you to think positive and write your own list of 10 affirmations on the template on the next page.

AFFIRMATIONS RULE

1. _____
   _____

2. _____
   _____

3. _____
   _____

4. _____
   _____

5. _____
   _____

6. _____
   _____

7. _____
   _____

8. _____
   _____

9. _____
   _____

10. _____
    _____

Chapter 2

Emotions

Emotions help us to experience the world and they allow us to have rich and meaningful engagement with our environment, our friends, our pets, and even our families. Even anger and frustration are great. When we are able to connect to what makes us angry and what leads to frustration, that can change how we approach a person, a situation, or an assignment. Emotions are not so great when we cannot break from feeling just one way or we just can't get off the loop of being angry, or the frustration never ends.

Emotions evolve and are a part of development. What does that mean? Well, think about how a 2-year-old reacts to not getting what they want. Now think about how an 8-year-old reacts, a 14-year-old, and now a 22-year-old. Ideally, there should be a big difference between these people. I'm sure you're thinking "I know some adults who act like they are 2." You're right, you do.

Learning to cope with complex feelings, like frustration, is a vital part of development and an important part of well-being. When a 2-year-old is mad, he is mad. He may know why he is mad (I didn't get that toy) but he probably cannot explain it to you. An 8-year-old will be able to tell you. A 14-year-old can probably have a discussion about being hurt or confused, and a 22-year-old may be able to clarify why they had such a reaction, based on previous experiences or certain ideas.

This change in approach and engagement is as much a part of brain and body development as it is a part of psychological development.

The teen brain is "in progress." The human brain grows rapidly when a child is born and gets to about 80 percent of adult size by the time that a kid is about 2–3 years old. The brain continues to mature in your teen years, until your mid-20s, and these years are vital for brain development. That means that, although the human brain may not get a lot bigger, there is still a lot of change that is happening.

The brain is a complex system of cells and pathways that form networks. These cells and networks "talk" to each other through chemical signals. As you grow, you may use some groups of cells more, such as the ones that help you learn new things, like playing tennis. As we use certain groups more often, we strengthen those connections or networks and over time we start becoming better and better at the tasks that we do most often. In addition, our ability to learn complex information gets better.

For example, you may have thought that addition was hard when you were 5, but over time that gets easier and you start building on knowledge and start doing more and more complex mathematics such as multiplication, division, and eventually work up to things like algebra. This process involves learning and practice and is related to brain maturation and development.

Your brain is one of the most sophisticated systems ever made and, like any great system, proper maintenance is required. Some of this is related to challenging yourself with experiences and information. That being said, if you don't have high-quality nutrition, your system may not be as complex or quick as you want. High-quality, balanced nutrition is the foundation for a healthy and powerful brain and its networks.

We want our brain and body functions to be at their best so that we feel at our best. Emotions are some of the best parts of who we are. However, as we mentioned above, emotions can be problematic when we get caught in them.

Puberty and the teen years can be filled with emotional ups and downs and part of that is related to the various biological and hormonal changes that are going on in the body. Despite the fact that adolescence is the time when we start questioning our environment and simple answers are not enough anymore, some of the areas of the brain that help us with the most with complex decision making and emotional regulation are still developing.

That doesn't mean that teens cannot regulate themselves or that they don't have incredibly complex thoughts, but it does mean that sometimes decisions can be based more on emotions. Researchers did this study where they had a group of teen drivers and a group of adult drivers participate in a simulated driving task. The teen drivers and adult drivers had very similar driving skills when they initially tested them. Then the scientists did something really interesting. They had peers who were of similar age to the drivers observe them in the task, a little like having a friend in the car.[1] What do you think happened? Yup, you guessed it. The risk-taking behavior in the teen drivers went up. In another study, a group of teens and a group of adults were asked, "Do you want to swim with sharks?" The adults said "No" and the teens thought about it for a while before deciding. Admittedly, swimming with sharks sounds really cool to all of us too, but the point is that teens are more willing to take risks and sometimes their decisions can be based more on emotions versus facts. That doesn't mean that adults don't do that too. We already know that you know adults who act like 2-year-olds, but, in general, adults will have less emotional reactivity to a situation.

We are not saying that adults always make better decisions; what we are saying is that pausing and thinking about how you are feeling and reacting in a moment might help you to better manage the situation in front of you, in other words *check yourself before you wreck yourself*. It's normal to seek stimulating experiences and challenge the world around you, especially in the teen years. As you explore ways to live life and challenge yourself, we would like to suggest channeling that great energy into something like adventure sports and getting involved in a passion project (writing, art, science, travel, whatever) versus going off the rails with activities that could hurt your health and development (substance use, reckless behaviors, etc.).

Hormonal shifts happen as well. *The Female Brain* and *The Male Brain* author Dr. Louann Brizendine says the teen female brain will experience estrogen-progesterone surges that will activate oxytocin (driving them toward social bonding—hence the trips to the bathroom with their girlfriends to talk). The teen male brain increases in testosterone and vasopressin—driving them to focus on things like the pecking order and the need for respect, which has been shown to decrease talking.[2]

These hormonal changes increase the need to be desired in most individuals, but it's important to stay in touch with your own desires during this stage, like what makes you happy, rather than just the need to be desired. If we understand this is biology, and just one part of who we are, we can work to reshape thoughts through various skills and tools. You will be learning about these tools and skills in this chapter as well as the chapters to come. We, as humans, are "in progress" and our brains and bodies are experiencing a lot of change. The teen years are all about change, emotional and physical, and, in many ways, we humans are very malleable and flexible during this time.

Pros and Cons

Thoughts can sometimes feel like the glitter in a snow globe—plentiful, scattered, and easily shaken up. The short-term goal or the instant thought about a decision can feel good, but how long does that really last in most cases? Creating a pros and cons list can help with anchoring ideas. This exercise is like setting the snow globe down on a table, making the mind more clear for the answer.

Start by creating a pros and cons list in the blank space provided after our sample. By putting each on paper you may be able to answer the question "Is this really something that works for me?" We encourage you to practice using pros and cons for simple decisions, like whether or not try out for a team, and make your way to bigger topics like where to go to college.

We have chosen to use texting and driving as a sample. Most teens have to take this situation on at some point. We are asking you to think through it in a meaningful way, but please also keep in mind that texting and driving is banned in many places and this is not a question to be pondered but a law that has to be followed for everyone's safety.

Pros of Texting While Driving

- I want to, I really, really want to.

- My phone distracts me and I don't have to think about other stuff that is stressful or negative.

- I wouldn't be leaving my friends hanging without an answer from me.

- It's a habit, it's easier to do it than not do it.

- I do it all the time and it's fine because nothing's happened yet.

- It's so instinctive that I don't even know that I'm doing it until after I start texting. (Maybe not so much of a pro if you ask us. See the last point in the cons.)

Cons of Texting While Driving

- I could kill or hurt someone else.

- I could get hurt or killed. [Car crashes are the leading cause of death for teen drivers and distracted driving is one of the biggest reasons why. Texting and driving increases your risk of a crash 23 times.]

- I might have to pull over[3] (to be safe) and this may make me late to where I'm going. My friends might get mad at me for not responding or being late (even though it's always been fine and people understand, just like I would).

- I may have to put my phone away because I can't stop myself from grabbing it, but I don't want to put it away.

- I'm so zoned out that I pick my phone and before I know it, I'm texting. I'm not really paying attention to the road.

PROS AND CONS

Pros

_____

_____

_____

_____

Cons

_____

_____

_____

_____

Pros

_____

_____

_____

_____

Cons

_____

_____

_____

_____

Name that Feeling

A growing body of research has revealed that labeling an emotion, or putting feelings into words, reduces the intensity of the emotion. Emotions are important indicators that something needs attending to, but they don't always make sense, and they don't need to.

For example, if you feel guilty because you just robbed a bank, that guilt is there to signal you to take the money back and make amends. But if you feel guilt for no reason, do your best not to add a story to it, it may be "unjustified guilt." Note that it's not uncommon to have two emotions at the same time, for example, your friend may have received an "A" on a test while you received a "B." You can feel happy for her and a bit envious at the same time, this is called "mixed emotion."

The ability to label the emotions accurately will provide some relief. This technique will reduce suffering but the emotion you are experiencing might still be painful, just not as intense as it would be otherwise. In the exercise below, do your best to label your current emotional state, make note of a thought you notice, and describe any bodily sensation.

Look at the two examples we have provided below to see how this technique works. Now write down descriptions of your feelings, bodily sensations and thoughts you notice as if you were observing them from afar.

There is a feeling of restlessness in me right now. I just noticed a thought about wishing I didn't have to study for finals today. My bodily sensation is low energy.

There is a feeling of anxiety in me right now. A thought about not wanting to get up and speak in front of the class just popped up for me. Bodily sensation is heart palpitating.

NAME THAT FEELING

1. _____
   _____
   _____
   _____
   _____
   _____
   _____
   _____
   _____

2. _____
   _____
   _____
   _____
   _____
   _____
   _____
   _____

Chapter 3

Learning Our Stress System

The material in this chapter can get a little technical, but we think you'll find it really useful to understand. Understanding the stress system is central to eating mindfully in modern society, so stay tuned here to learn about what "chilling out" has to do with eating in the most optimal way, and a whole lot of other things too.

Stress is not just some imaginary thing, it's a very real physical experience. It is well cited that the most universal fear is public speaking. So, for example, we start with an idea ("I'm scared of speaking in front of the class") and we have bodily sensations such as our heart racing, cheeks flushing, and our hands shaking. Why does this physical response happen when we are merely thinking about something stressful? Let us introduce the autonomic nervous system (ANS).

We've only been in the know about our ANS since the early 1900s, when the term "fight or flight" was first coined. Back in the day, stress was a term used when discussing mathematics or physics, the force of one object on another. What we finally started looking at in science is how the force of our thoughts impacts our bodies—and the idea of stress as we know it was born.

Humans have a very physical response to threat. If a tiger is chasing you, you run (flight) or fight...or maybe you have an immobility response, known as freeze. We are all unique and there is no one way to get stressed. That being said, since our autonomic nervous system is the same, a lot of people feel the same stuff when they get nervous or anxious or scared.

However, exactly how stress "shows up" can be different for all of us. For example, many people get headaches. Others get stomach aches. Most people will tell you that they feel like their heart is beating really fast or their hands get shaky. All totally normal. The reason that we feel these things is that one part of our ANS, the sympathetic nervous system, is in protection mode. Yup, your nervous system is trying to protect you, it's just that it is often doing the right thing at the wrong time. Your mind knows the difference between a tiger chasing you and your mid-term paper that is due in 2 days, your body's stress response may not. A threat is a threat and your body is going to find a way to deal with it. So, it raises your blood pressure to get more blood to your muscles and vital organs, and does it as fast as possible by increasing your heart rate. Your pupils dilate to let in more light so that you can see, and a lot of other things happen. Cool, right?

Well, cool, only in short bursts and if it is managed well to help push us to stay up later to get a paper done. We are not made to be in a constant state of "go go go." Your sympathetic system is your friend but, if it is overused, it may become a friend that is making your life harder and less fun.

Our body likes balance and our sympathetic system is balanced by our parasympathetic nervous system (PNS). The PNS is that part of our ANS that helps us to rest and helps us to have a lower heart rate and more relaxed muscles. When we are at rest we are more comfortable, and when we are more comfortable our system is able to digest and metabolize food better because we are not using our energy to flee or fight a threat. Your PNS sets the stage for connected eating as well—when your mind is in a state of calm, it can listen closely to your body's cues like when to eat, what to eat, and when to stop. Kinda hard to tune in and decide from the inside when to eat, what to eat, and when to stop, when you are focused on not being eaten yourself. The cool thing is that you have the power to change your stress response.

Mindfulness techniques come in handy for conditioning the ANS—you might have noticed that it's trendy right now. Well, unlike selfie sticks and friendship bracelets, it's a timeless trend we doubt will ever truly go away. What is mindfulness? It's paying attention to what's going on right now and not thoughts about what happened before or what's going to happen next week. It's about trying to be in the moment so that you are not freaking yourself out about a lot of stuff that isn't actually happening right now. For example, if you are stressing about that report that's due on Monday and you know that your stomach is hurting because you're so worried, you probably need to remind yourself that it's Saturday afternoon. Sometimes, we get so fixated on what we think is going to happen, we forget that that thing is not actually happening right now. The point of mindfulness is not to make you forget that you have a report due on Monday, it's to help you realize that right now it's Saturday and by taking a deep breath you can cool off that stress response and slow down your heart rate and blood pressure. By helping yourself calm down, you will be able to focus better on what you can do to get a plan in place for how to get that report done. So, you see that it's not magic, but understanding how to help yourself when you feel that the tiger maybe coming after you.

Below are some mindfulness skills for handling stress that just take a snap-of-a-finger. The goal is for stressors in your life to not equal stress for you.

Daily Drive-Thru: Mindfulness Commitment

The concept of Drive-Thru Spirituality recognizes how busy you are and that the pace of modern living isn't slowing down anytime soon. Even a few minutes of a mindfulness practice are better than none. The benefits of these short exercises sort of sneak up on you. Start off with "child-size" drive-thru commitments such as these:

- I will commit to taking 5–10 deep breaths when I wake up each morning to get centered and grounded. Taking deep breaths is a quick way to activate the PNS because it slows the stress response, which slows your heart rate and lowers your blood pressure and that can make it easier to think more clearly and make a more calm and focused choice (besides, your breath is always with you, so it's ridiculously convenient).

- Every night before bed I will set a timer for 3 minutes and practice letting my thoughts come and go as if they're cars passing by my house.

- I will enjoy my own company and do something simple that I like, like laying in the grass or drawing or painting. I'll try to keep my thoughts with the activity that I am doing.

Mindless Versus Mindful: Reassessing Your Spare Time

Most of us look for ways to relax after a stressful day. For some people, this means heading straight to the Xbox when they get home. Others login to their Instagram account. Start paying attention to what you do when you want to quiet your mental noise, then consider swapping a mindless activity for a mindful one. There's a time and a place for mindless activities (we don't need to make them a big deal) but, if done excessively, they don't exactly deliver what they promise. In other words, Xboxing for hours at a time may give you an illusion of rejuvenation but it doesn't truly make you feel rested.

It's kind of like a counterfeit mindfulness. Counterfeit mindfulness is like counterfeit money—it looks good, but you can't buy anything with it. True mindfulness is more about checking *in* than it is about checking *out*. How do you feel after 4 hours of Xboxing? Alert, aware, and focused or checked out? We are guessing checked out, and this is usually the opposite of being alert, aware, and focused.

Often people are not getting rejuvenated when they do mindless activities for long periods of time. Checking out for a little while is great, but checking out because you don't know how else to cope is not the best way to deal with it. Checking out will help you temporarily put your worries on the shelf, but they will eventually play Jack-in-the-box on you. You are better off facing the situation right off the bat.

The difference between mindfulness, or checking in with what's stressing you out, is that you can deal with the situation if you're willing to pay attention to what's actually going on. Playing Xbox all weekend and avoiding the paper will not make the assignment go away. We know it's scary to face the deadline that's coming up. We are not saying it's always going to be easy, but you can handle it. By taking a deep breath and recognizing that you are avoiding the situation, you might be able to come up with a schedule for completing your paper or talk to a friend or your parents and ask for some help with the assignment.

Practice Noticing an Experience
with and without Mindfulness

Noticing what is going on in your own body and mind (being mindful) when stuff happens can give you a lot information about how to approach the situation. Shifting your feelings from reacting to observing may help. The difference between noticing something and reacting to it is usually the emotions that we attach to the situation. Mindfulness is the difference between being in the middle of a corn maze versus getting an aerial view of it. It's the same situation but a clearer vantage point.

Read the client samples below and notice the difference between those samples that use mindfulness tools and those that don't. Think about what approach might work best for you. Now get an aerial view and "notice" the same situation. Take the charge out of it.

Washing the dishes without mindfulness: I hate washing the dishes. I have all of these dishes to do. There are so many, it's going to take forever. Washing the dishes is the worst thing ever, why do I always have to wash them?

Washing the dishes with mindfulness: I notice a thought of having to do "all" the dishes. I will focus my attention back to the thought of doing "one" dish at a time. The water temperature feels so hot at first I can feel my teeth clenching. As the water temperature has just the right balance of hot/cold I notice my facial expression relaxing. The suds are thick and smell like lavender, and it reminds me of a fragrance I've smelled before. The dishes feel slippery in my hands from the suds. I notice a thought in my head about how sparkly the dishes look when I'm done. I like that it gives me a sense of completion: there is a beginning, a middle, and an end.

Classroom without mindfulness: I do not want to be here. I cannot wait for class to get out, I hate math and I'm never going to get it. I wish I could just be at the skate park with my friends all day. Every minute in this class feels like an eternity.

Classroom with mindfulness: I just noticed a thought of wanting to go to the skate park after school. I'm physically in the classroom, but mentally at the skate park. I'll bring my attention back to the present moment and do my best to "throw myself in" so I'm not lost on what we are supposed to be doing for homework. I'll do my best to cultivate curiosity about the subject I'm learning.

PRACTICE NOTICING AN EXPERIENCE WITH AND WITHOUT MINDFULNESS

An experience without mindfulness: _____

_____

_____

_____

_____

_____

_____

An experience with mindfulness: _____

_____

_____

_____

_____

_____

_____

An experience without mindfulness: _____

_____

_____

_____

_____

_____

_____

An experience with mindfulness: _____

_____

_____

_____

_____

_____

_____

Mindfulness Inventory

Okay, time for inventory. How often do you check out? Make a list and get real with yourself about the mindFUL and mindLESS activities in your life. Get to know when you zone out. As we have mentioned before, we recognize the value of down time and needing to tune out for a while. That being said, how often are you really doing that? Do you find yourself doing that way too often? An inventory is a great way to become aware of the behaviors we engage in, giving us a choice about whether or not we want to change them. Use the blank lines to fill in some of your own.

MINDFULNESS INVENTORY

Mindful Activities

1. Reading a book

2. Going for a walk

3. Playing with your pet

4. Helping your parents prep for dinner

5. Washing the dishes

6. _____

7. _____

8. _____

9. _____

10. _____

Mindless Activities

1. YouTubing for hours

2. Incessantly checking your technology for notifications

3. Eating when you're bored, on a regular basis

4. Facebook

5. Binge-watching Netflix

6. _____

7. _____

8. _____

9. _____

10. _____

You're GROUNDED!

Associating letters and words can help with remembering them. Use this acronym as an easy memory tool to remind yourself about being mindful.

Get your groove on; adopt a mindfulness movement like aikido, yoga, or walking a labyrinth.

Relax by taking 10 deep breaths.

Opt out of unhelpful thoughts and opt in to being a little more kind to yourself.

Unplug and give yourself a needed break from all the stimulation.

Navigate away from ruminating about the past or worrying about the future.

Desire to do activities that rejuvenate.

Eat when calm and (if you can) sit down and give yourself a rest.

Discover what's going on around you, and observe the color on the wall or the sound of the room that you are in.

Chapter 4

Get Your ZZZZZZs!

There is no shortcut to sleep, unfortunately, you can't have someone sleep for you. When you don't sleep it throws life out of balance, including how and what you eat. Lack of sleep can alter your hunger and satiety hormones, making it difficult to identify natural hunger cues and fullness.[1] It's true, sleep and connected eating are linked, and when we are tired we may end up "feeding tired." When sleep deprived, we are less connected to our body. First, we tend to eat mindlessly while tired with less attention to what we are choosing. Second, you may end up "feeding tired"—just trying to eat for energy to keep you awake (like grabbing a cup of coffee to keep you going). Basically, when we are tired, we make different choices and often those are not the balanced choices we would make if we were rested.

> *There's no way that you need a pint of ice cream to satisfy a craving; if a few spoonfuls or a dish doesn't do the trick, then ice cream isn't what you were craving to begin with.*
>
> Karen Koenig[2]

Karen Koenig, author of *The Rules of "Normal" Eating*, is basically saying that a craving should result in the original desire becoming less. Some people find they have a lot more cravings when they are tired. But ask yourself, what are you really hungry for? Most would say, "energy." The truth is that you get that energy by allowing your system to rest and get some sleep. However, what do we actually do when we are tired? We grab a cup of coffee or an energy drink or some munchies to keep ourselves going. This may work in the moment, but it's just a band-aid, it only works for a short time. You were really craving rest; coffee just masks the fatigue. So, you may have had the coffee, maybe even wanted the coffee, and maybe even enjoyed the coffee, but that wasn't the original craving and you likely feel the same "tired" a short time later. The real need was sleep.

ARE YOU SLEEP DEPRIVED?

Below is a quiz to test whether you are sleep deprived. Answer each question with a "true" or a "false."

True or false?	Sleep statement
	I need an alarm clock to wake me up at the appropriate time.
	It's a struggle for me to get out of bed in the morning.
	Weekday mornings I hit the snooze bar several times to get more sleep.
	I feel tired, irritable, and stressed out during the week.
	I have trouble concentrating and remembering.
	I feel slow with critical thinking, problem solving, and being creative. I often fall asleep watching TV.
	I often fall asleep in boring meetings or lectures or in warm rooms.
	I often fall asleep after heavy meals.
	I often fall asleep while relaxing after dinner.
	I often fall asleep within 5 minutes of getting into bed.
	I often feel drowsy while driving.
	I often sleep extra hours on weekend mornings.
	I often need a nap to get through the day.
	I have dark circles around my eyes.

Tally up the number of "trues." If you answered "true" to any three of the above questions, consider yourself sleep deprived![3]

Don't worry, you're not alone in feeling exhausted. Teenagers happen to be the most sleep-deprived population in the entire world! Maybe you're thinking you can just catch up on sleep later, like on the weekend? Sorry to burst your bubble, but that's not how it works.

Catch-up sleep is a bit of a myth. Even if one catches up on the weekend, that does not negate the damage to attentiveness, short-term memory, school and work errors, accidents, exam results, impacted by the sleep deprivation that occurred in real time. If people catch up on their sleep, and appear to get back to baseline, they still can't change the past. Think of it this way, you can't just plan to fill the car up on Saturday when the fuel gauge is telling you the tank's empty now and it's Wednesday. You're going to end up stranded on a road somewhere walking to a gas station. Unless you're Fred Flintstone who basically runs his caveman car to work and therefore doesn't need gas, or wheels for that matter. Your sleep deprivation is like the physics of Fred's feet, it doesn't work.[4] There is no shortcut, the only way you catch up on sleep is by creating a stable sleep pattern and getting a consistent amount of sleep on a regular basis.

HOW MUCH SLEEP DO YOU GET A NIGHT? ALLY'S STORY: 15 YEARS OLD

During the weekdays, I sleep from 9pm till 6am. A lot of my friends think I'm crazy because I go to sleep so early, but I can't function without that much sleep. Of course, I get on my phone when I should be sleeping. If I wake up during the night the first thing I do is check my notifications. This usually prevents me from being able to fall asleep again quickly. Over the weekend I stay up later because I don't have school to worry about, like I'll get to sleep at 12am and won't wake up until 10am the next morning.

If you are getting less than 6 hours of sleep a night, you are 4 times more likely to get a cold,[5] you are more likely to be at a higher weight than you would be if you were well rested, and lack of sleep makes your brain foggy. Having a foggy mind isn't a helpful tool in school, life, sports, or most other things that you probably care about. Not getting enough sleep can literally make you...ummmm, not your smartest self.

Oh, and by the way, it also affects your mood. When we don't feel right we try to find a reason for it, we forget that the reason may be fatigue, and, as a result, we become more attracted to bad news. Feelings of sadness, depression, and irritability can be made more severe, and concentration can be more difficult, if you're not getting enough sleep. Now imagine how much worse those and other mood issues become when sleep deprivation becomes chronic. There's a reason they use sleep deprivation in warfare. It's not exactly a mood enhancer. So, don't go to war on your body; peace out when bedtime arrives and just do it. You're not Fred Flintstone with flaming feet; running on empty would give you nothing but "road rash."

It's true that teens and young adults have a natural shift in their biological sleep rhythm (also known as the circadian rhythm). Teens shift to a slightly longer circadian cycle and the pressure to go to sleep shifts to a later time. So, you may start noticing that you don't feel sleepy until 11pm whereas you used to feel sleepy around 9pm. This desire to sleep later is very natural and so is the need to sleep in. Basically, teens want to sleep later and wake up later.

However, the demands of life, school, and other activities don't allow for us to keep this kind of sleep schedule. Unfortunately, what happens is that teens stay up late, due to this natural drive that makes it harder to go to sleep, or because they are doing homework, or because they are out with friends; but they still have to get up early. The time for a full night's rest gets compressed. So, even though teens should be getting at least 8–9 hours of sleep a night (athletes about 9.25 hours), they actually get maybe 7 hours, and often less than that. Sleep can be even more important in your teen years than at other stages of life. As we have discussed in other chapters in this book, the teen years are a key growth time and sleep is a really important part of healthy growth and development.

LUCAS ON SLEEP AND SNAPCHAT: 14 YEARS OLD

My sleep schedule varies. I'm supposed to put my phone in another room at 9pm on weekdays, but I don't end up doing that until 10pm or 10:30pm some nights. I'll usually wake up at 6:20am and jump in the shower really quickly, 'cause I don't usually take one the night before after practice like I'm supposed to, and go back to sleep again until 7:15am. On a weekend, if I don't have a game, I'll stay up on Snapchat until no one else is awake.

LIGHTS OUT AND MEME ACCOUNTS: JACK'S STORY: 13 YEARS OLD

I go into my room at 9pm to go to bed, but I get on my phone to play games or login to my meme Instagram account for about a half hour before I go to bed. Don't tell my dad.

Technology is part of our lives and it has improved how we live, learn, and travel in the world. Overall, tech is great. But, tech has really messed with our sleep. Teens get less sleep because they stay up later, using their devices. Teens spend a mind-boggling 9 hours per day on tech, with some 13-year-olds checking social media 100 times per day.[6] Nine hours is more than most teens are sleeping at night! All this tech competes with sleep time. Teens can struggle to go into the deeper stages of sleep because their mind is awake and waiting for that next text, update, message, or whatever else. Even the light in our gadgets can stimulate our brain and keep us awake. Light is a major disruptor of an important sleep hormone called melatonin. Melatonin helps us to fall asleep and when our bodies and brains are too stimulated by light, melatonin secretion can be suppressed, disrupting our sleep. There are now apps that help to reduce the blue light in your computers, iPad, and phones for this very reason. But, even better, would be to take the tech out of your bedroom, like down the hall!

Another important sleep disruptor is caffeine. To really get enough sleep, it's important to watch caffeine consumption. Too much caffeine, timed incorrectly, can make it impossible to fall asleep because caffeine is a stimulant. It revs your system up. Research shows 75 percent of kids today are consuming caffeine, and the more caffeine someone consumes, the less sleep they get.[7] Caffeinated drinks like sodas, or good old-fashioned coffee or tea, will take 4–8 hours to leave your system (depends on a person's individual metabolism of caffeine). We suggest not having caffeine after 2–3pm because it will still be in your system as you get ready to go to bed. Even decaf coffee can have a little caffeine. And don't even get us started on energy drinks! Rockstar energy drinks won't leave you feeling much like a rock star when you're lying awake at night freaking out because you know you're going to feel like a zombie the next day. They don't give you real energy as much as a temporary burst of stimulation which can cause an increase in your heart rate and blood pressure, among other things. So it's not real or sustained energy and we are back at the core concept of "What is your body really asking for?" If you are looking for real and lasting energy, you don't have to look far, 'cause it's sleep.

Sleep Hygiene

Your sleep hygiene is your routine for taking care of your body's sleep needs. How attentive are you to listening to the cues when you are feeling tired? Getting yourself off to bed on time and up at a regular time is a life skill that will enhance your life immensely by improving your mood, preventing disconnected eating, and enhancing your performance, focus, and ability to learn.

Ways to Improve Sleep[8]

- Establish a regular sleep/wake schedule. Go to bed at the same time and wake up at the same time each day.

- Avoid drinking fluids right before bed; you might find you have to go to the bathroom in the middle of the night. And if you are peeing, you are not sleeping!

- Get continuous sleep: it's not okay to sleep 4 hours at night and 4 hours after school. That doesn't lead to high-quality restorative sleep.

- If you want to nap, choose a "power nap" which is a quick 30-minute nap. Set an alarm and try to avoid marathon long naps which will disrupt nighttime sleep (making it hard for you to fall or stay asleep).

- Aim to have a dark, cool, uncluttered room. Put away your laptops, papers, and phones before turning in for the night.

- Reduce "blue light" at night. Using smartphones, tablets, and computers at night can stimulate your brain and suppress melatonin, making it harder to fall asleep. To block these blue lights, try using orange tinted glasses or apps that reduce the blue lights from devices.

- Establish a soothing bedtime ritual to help you fall asleep. Take a warm bath, do some gentle stretching, or read a book or magazine. Avoid reading on your phone.

- Keep the bed for sleep. Don't eat, do homework, or use tech in bed. Your mind needs to associate your bed with rest and not homework.

Sleep Disorders

Sometimes there are medical reasons why someone is not able to sleep well. We are not going to review every one of these conditions, but we do feel that it is important for you to know that there are sleep disorders such as sleep apnea (not being able to breathe well while sleeping and more common among snorers) or narcolepsy (excessive daytime sleepiness, sometimes with sudden episodes of falling asleep or "sleep attacks"), among others, that can lead to excessive fatigue and very dysregulated sleep. Additionally, chronic health conditions such as asthma, depression, and diabetes, to name a few, can also cause sleep problems. If you feel that you have tried the sleep hygiene suggestions but are still struggling to sleep, it may be time to talk with your doctor.

TAKING STOCK OF YOUR SLEEP HYGIENE

Make a list below of the common characteristics you see in your own sleep hygiene. Looking at your answers can highlight areas you need to work on:

1. _____
_____
_____

2. _____
_____
_____

3. _____
_____
_____

4. _____
_____
_____

5. _____
_____
_____

6. _____
_____
_____

7. _____
_____
_____

CREATING A SLEEP RITUAL

Create a sleep plan. Pick three ways in which you can improve your sleep. This could be creating a regular bedtime and wake time regardless of weekends or weekdays. It could be turning off all tech 1–2 hours before sleep. It could also be to make your bed clutter-free. Try and identify three things that you think would help and see if you can do them for 3 days, for starters:

1. _____
_____
_____
_____
_____
_____

2. _____
_____
_____
_____
_____
_____

3. _____
_____
_____
_____
_____
_____

Chapter 5

Exercise

Someday, when you're a bit older, you'll inevitably hear the Confucius quote, "Choose a job you love, and you will never have to work a day in your life." This is how we feel about exercise. The term "working out" has gotten a bad rap because it implies that exercise is like a chore.

Similar to moving your body, if you've ever jumped on your beach cruiser when you're in a bad mood, you'll find that it's impossible to stay bummed out. Most people would agree that including exercise regularly helps to keep them happy. Literally. But the key is to find exercise you love.

During exercise, endorphins (hormones) are released which can provide what's known as an "all-natural high." This feeling can last several hours after exercise is finished. It might initially be challenging to incorporate more intentional movement into your life if you have not done so in the past. However, you are likely to notice several benefits of exercise soon after you begin. Specifically, exercise not only can improve mood, but it helps you to reduce stress, sleep better at night, pay attention in school, and helps to keep your emotions in check.

The Benefits of Moving

- Improves mood, makes you happy.

- Keeps emotions stable.

- Reduces stress, clears cortisol.

- Improves cognitive concentration.

- Helps with sleep.

- Strengthens your heart, muscles, and tendons.

- Fine-tunes your hunger/satiety cues.

- Improves coordination.

- Gives sense of self-mastery.

- Increases ability to learn and retain new information.

- Provides an opportunity to try out new activities.

- Is an opportunity to socialize with others.

- Practices becoming aware of, and adjusting your effort/ intensity.

- Builds immune system, decreasing likelihood of injury or illness.

Although you might think that you are invincible, research has shown that you are more likely to live a longer, healthier life (and become even more invincible) if you include physical activity.[1] Our bodies come in all different shapes and sizes, so, rather than focusing on your weight to improve your health, your long-term health and wellness will be more apt to improve if you regularly engage in physical activities that you enjoy.

This means participating in a variety of enjoyable activities while taking into consideration responsibilities in your life, rather than structuring your life around exercise. Sport psychologist Dr. Riley Nickols calls this balanced exercise.

Signs that You Have a Balanced Relationship with Exercise

- You are able to listen to your body and respond appropriately. This might result in feeling up to moving some days and feeling as though rest is needed on other days.

- You participate in activities with internal goals like the expectation of fun versus external goals such as weight loss.

- You see your exercise as flexible, meaning that you might need to adjust your workouts when school, social, or family commitments arise—for example, you don't expect to workout 4 days a week during finals.

- You allow your body to rest, knowing that rest will not diminish your desire to exercise on other days.[2]

- You eat enough food to adequately fuel your level of activity.

- Exercise changes with the seasons (for example, in the rainy season you may increase yoga and decrease soccer).

There is also "unbalanced exercise." The warning signs are either observable to others or happening within an individual.

Signs that You Have an Unbalanced Relationship with Exercise

- The gym is on fire but you have two minutes left on the treadmill, so you stay on.

- You feel anxious if you don't get to do your workout on a particular day.

- You think of working out as a way to make up for what you ate.

- You work out even when you are sick, injured, or tired.

- You are working out to delay physical changes to your body.

- You work out for external goals only (physical appearance).

- You work out in odd places at odd times.

- You don't eat enough for the energy you are expending.

- Your family or friends have expressed concern that you are exercising too much.

- You force yourself to exercise even when you do not feel like doing so.

- You often miss out on attending social or family gatherings as a result of your workouts.

To assess if you have an unbalanced relationship with exercising, feel free to check out the Compulsive Exercise Test from *Almost Anorexic* (see the Resources section of this book). If you find that several of these warning signs apply to you, it is recommended that you seek professional help to better understand your relationship with exercise and to explore how you might be able to be more flexible and spontaneous.

As previously mentioned, there are a multitude of benefits of moving regularly throughout your life. However, some individuals have difficulty consistently incorporating physical activity while others entirely avoid physical activity. There are many reasons why an individual might abstain from moving, including: not finding enjoyment in exercise, feeling uncomfortable moving in his or her body, lack of confidence or experience in trying out new activities.

If you've been avoiding exercise for some of the reasons stated above, you might benefit from dipping your toe in the water. Avoidance of a particular activity maintains the fear of it. If the last time you exercised was uncomfortable, and you decided afterward to never go again, it will remain that way in your head.

Consider the Goldilocks Approach (see more below), where the goal is to find an activity that is not "too hot" (trying out for the NFL), or too cold (no activity at all), but that is just right, somewhere in the middle. We understand that challenging yourself may cause an increase in anxiety, but the good news is that a process called habituation occurs over time. Habituation is kind of like getting into a hot tub: at first, it's too hot, but after some time it's totally manageable. If you keep it up you could go from being a toe-dipper to a cannon-baller. You'll find that not only can the anxiety be tolerated, but it also decreases over time. A small amount of anxiety can actually set you free.

And what's cool is that lots of times when we head toward our fear, it's not as bad as you thought. The idea is to start by taking the next step in front of you. So, if friends ask you to play a casual game of soccer in the park, take that step by saying yes. Afterward, you might think, "Wow, playing soccer in the park with friends was actually really fun even though I didn't feel very good at it." Then do your best to run mental replays of the good parts of that experience for the next couple of days, like how nice it was to be included, or the ability to laugh at yourself for a mistake you made on the field. This will make it a little easier to be open to saying yes the next time. See the exposure hierarchy exercises below to rate activities you've avoided because they caused you anxiety or made you uncomfortable.

SUSIE ON JOYFUL MOVEMENT: 16 YEARS OLD

Susie definitely wasn't an athlete. She spent most of her time reading or studying. She had too many eggs in one basket, even though it was a good basket. It was like having a house full of plants but only watering one all of the time. She decided it would be a good idea to distribute some eggs to a different basket. Therefore, she wanted to introduce some type of movement into her life to reduce stress and help her to sleep better at night. First, she observed a Taekwondo class, but decided it might be awkward to ask someone to go nunchucking with her on the weekends. Next, she bought a lacrosse stick, before actually knowing if she liked lacrosse. Finally, she started taking tennis lessons and her tennis instructor eventually encouraged her to join the tennis team. It was then that she fell in love with the sport. Justin Bieber could have shown up at her tennis club to take her out, and she would have declined if it was in the middle of a match. She loved the camaraderie, the competition, and moving in a way that didn't feel like "working out." Susie stated that tennis makes her happier, even when she's studying. It quiets her mind, grounds her, and helps her manage her stress.

Getting in the Groove of Moving

Another reason an individual may not be moving at all could be that they are simply out of the habit of moving. We have evolved to have habits so that we can expend energy doing other things. Can you imagine having to learn to brush your teeth all over again, every single morning? With the mind's ability to form a habit we can brush our teeth and be doing other things, like brushing your teeth while going to the bathroom (maybe don't post it though), aka multitasking.

Dr. B. Timothy Walsh, from the Columbia Center for Eating Disorders, states that once behaviors get linked together into a routine, and once the chain of action is initiated, the rest follows with little mental effort.[3] Yet sometimes habits take hold when they are not useful. So, if you were trying to break a bad habit, that's called "habit reversal" (more on habit reversal in Chapter 11). Creating a new habit is called "habit formation." Habit formation is the process by which new behaviors become automatic. If you feel inclined to lace up your tennis shoes and hit the courts as soon as you get home from school, you've acquired a habit. At first it takes a lot of effort to create a new automatic habit, but if you persist, it will become effortless, just like brushing your teeth.

Let's say that you used to love to play soccer on the soccer team, but you got burnt out and it's been a couple of years since you played, and you are now pretty sedentary. It doesn't mean we are suggesting you go from not moving for two years to joining the soccer team next week. We would first suggest you consult with a knowledgable parent, coach, or professional for how to implement a plan that will allow you to increase your activity in a safe and appropriate manner. If it has been challenging for you to be more active, it could be helpful to involve a parent or friend to join and encourage you to engage in more deliberate and intentional movement. This will likely require what we call "action precedes motivation." In other words, don't wait to get in the mood to move, move first, to get you in the mood. Once you've done something like routine walks/runs with your bestie and you have a sense of self-mastery, you've initiated habit formation.

Once the habit of moving is back in the mix, it's important to explore other aspects that will help you sustain movement. First, you will want to explore your last frame of reference of movement. Was soccer something you really enjoyed, or, in the end, were you doing it for your coach? If you really didn't like it, it's important to explore some different types of exercise to see what floats your boat. For some people, they would rather do almost anything else (including going to the dentist or pulling weeds) instead of going for a run. The monotonous nature of running or the discomfort the body might feel from continually pounding the pavement can be understandable deterrents for some people to enjoy running. However, others would jump at the opportunity to play a pick-up basketball game or go on a hike in the woods. The camaraderie and competition that basketball provides or taking in beautiful scenery on a hike in the woods are both helpful to engage in physical activity without feeling as though it is hard work! It's about finding exercise you love, so you never exercise a day in your life.

Second, some people are aware of the positive reasons they wish to exercise, but not aware of the negative reasons they wish not to. Wendy had a client who wanted to start moving more, but she was so annoyed by the non-stop badgering from her father that it made her want to do the opposite. She was ultimately shooting herself in the foot because she wanted to move, but she had been unable to separate the power play with her father from her desire to move. After she was able to cultivate an enjoyment for moving that was entirely her own, rather than to appease her father's demands, she was able to reignite her passion and enjoyment for being active.

Body Awareness Exercise for Balanced Exercise

Our hope is that by taking the time to think about the answers to the questions here, writing them down and then reading them, you will develop an automatic way to make your decision to move or not move. As you might have noticed in this chapter we don't want you to "drive" yourself to move, but rather follow through with joy. And if you "choose" not to move, that's cool, just as long as you are mindful about how you speak to yourself about it (for example, saying things like "I'm lazy," does not serve you because it's not true). See the prompts we provided and fill in your own answers on the next page, keeping in mind that your responses will shift and change with your mental and physical state.

1. What type of movement inspires you versus tires you today?

   Going to yoga where it's warm inside inspires me. The thought of soccer practice tires me because it's cold outside.

2. How was your sleep last night?

   Less than 7 hours.

3. How would you describe your energy level?

   Energy level is moderately low because I had less than 7 hours of sleep last night.

4. How is your mood?

   Mood is moderately low, but I think doing some exercise anyway, will lift my mood, especially yoga since it is one way to rejuvenate in addition to going to bed early tonight.

5. Are you able to adjust, modify, or skip a planned workout if needed?

   Yes, I would not go if I felt too tired.

6. What type of movement would be nourishing to you today?

   Restorative yoga.

BODY AWARENESS EXERCISE
FOR BALANCED EXERCISE

1. What type of movement inspires you versus tires you today?

    _____
    _____
    _____
    _____
    _____
    _____
    _____

2. How was your sleep last night?

    _____
    _____
    _____
    _____
    _____
    _____
    _____

3. How would you describe your energy level?

    _____
    _____
    _____
    _____
    _____
    _____
    _____

4. How is your mood?

    _____

    _____

    _____

    _____

    _____

    _____

    _____

5. Are you able to adjust, modify, or skip a planned workout
    if needed?

    _____

    _____

    _____

    _____

    _____

    _____

    _____

6. What type of movement would be nourishing to you
    today?

    _____

    _____

    _____

    _____

    _____

    _____

    _____

The Goldilocks Approach to Exercise

First, make a list of the activities that are "too hot," in other words, activities that would be too much of a stretch for you to consider right now. Next, make a second list of activities that would be "too cold," meaning the activities that would not give you any discomfort, but you would remain stuck. In order to find a healthier level of comfort you have to be willing to first increase your discomfort. Last, make a list that feels just right. Just right, in this case, means the activities that cause a bit of discomfort, but not too much.

Here's an example:

Too Hot

- Running when it's 100 degrees outside.
- Training for a marathon.

Too Cold

- Telling myself I'll start later and watching TV instead.

Just Right

- Making a commitment to some type of joyful movement 3 times this week.
- Go shopping for comfortable exercise shoes and clothing.

THE GOLDILOCKS APPROACH TO EXERCISE

Too Hot

_____
_____
_____
_____
_____
_____
_____

Too Cold

_____
_____
_____
_____
_____
_____
_____

Just Right

_____
_____
_____
_____
_____
_____
_____

Exposure Hierarchies of Exercise

On the next page, make a list of 10 types of activities you might consider and rate each item on a scale of 1 to 100 for how much anxiety the exercise causes (1% = no anxiety, and 100% = complete anxiety). For example:

1. Running a marathon = 100%

2. Playing soccer with friends in the park = 50%

3. Signing up for a restorative yoga class = 20%

4. Trying out for a sports team = 100%

5. Saying yes to your friends who want to go for a hike = 30%

6. Walking around the block with your dog for 15 minutes = 10%

7. Walking around the block with your mother for 15 minutes = 15%

8. Bike riding to school = 25%

9. Taking a Zumba class = 15%

10. Joining a charity bike race with your friends = 60%

We hope this list will help provide you with some direction on which activities would be a realistic and possibly achievable starting place as you consider reintroducing movement back into your life.

EXPOSURE HIERARCHIES OF EXERCISE

1. _____
   _____

2. _____
   _____

3. _____
   _____

4. _____
   _____

5. _____
   _____

6. _____
   _____

7. _____
   _____

8. _____
   _____

9. _____
   _____

10. _____
    _____

Part II

The Essentials for Connected Eating

Chapter 6

Making Foods Equal in Availability

It's important to make foods not only equal in morality, but also equal in availability. Often our hunger requests are thwarted by limited options. So, it's key to prep for your appetite's varied cravings (see the 3 Ts in Chapter 8) by keeping alternatives available, and in portions that make sense for different times and situations. By planning ahead, you can manage your hunger. With this sort of planning, you can eat what your body is calling for, rather than what's easiest to grab.

Your parents may be in charge of packing your meals for school. If so, tell them what foods you like, what foods you want, and whether what they are packing for you is enough. If you are packing your own meals, then take the job seriously. You pack your phone, wallet, computer, and now we are asking you to pack your lunch and snacks for the day (it's okay if parents help!). This will keep you fueled throughout the day, giving your brain and muscles energy to function at their best.

Variety is important to make sure you are getting different nutrients each day. For example, if you always ate a banana, you might miss out on the Vitamin C found in an orange. Similarly, if you only ate chicken and turkey each day, you might miss out on the iron found in red meat. Variety also helps keep you from feeling bored with food. When we eat the same thing over and over again, we're more likely to throw it away, or skip part of it, causing us to feel ravenous at the end of the school day. Changing it up at lunchtime, will make it feel more exciting to eat. Remember that all foods can be part of a healthy diet, not just the so-called "healthy" ones. There is no one nutrient responsible for poor health, food is just one part of our overall health and well-being.

Guidelines for Putting Meals Together

All teens have a high energy requirement given they are still growing and developing. Requirements are even higher for an athlete since they are expending more energy. This makes eating regularly, every 3–4 hours, especially important to prevent you from eating from one end of the pantry clear across the entire house. This usually translates to: 3 meals and 2–3 snacks per day.

Balanced meals are recommended, with all food groups present (starch, protein, vegetables/fruit, dairy, and fats), for at least 3 meals a day (breakfast, lunch, and dinner) plus snacks. This will provide satiety while also giving you the nutrients your body needs to thrive academically and athletically. A balanced diet not only fuels your muscles, but also fuels your brain. This helps you to feel sharp and focused, with a higher level of concentration. Getting both proteins and carbs, for example, slows down the digestion and keeps blood sugars more stable, making you feel full for a longer period of time. Fueling your brain allows you to have greater focus, which is helpful when taking a test or even just when trying to think.

Balanced meals would ideally include the following:

- *Protein*: This includes chicken, turkey, tuna, ham, peanut butter, eggs, hummus, tofu, beans, or cheese. Protein will help to keep you full throughout the day and is important for muscle growth, repair, and synthesizing important enzymes in the body to help your body work. It is also used to make your nails and hair strong...cool, right?

- *Carbohydrates*: Add a carbohydrate source to help boost energy. This could be a sandwich, wrap, roll, rice, or pasta. Carbohydrates are your body's main source for fuel and will help to give your brain, heart, and muscles energy to perform.

- *Fruit/vegetables*: Add some "color" to the meal by adding either a fruit or vegetable or both! Fruits and vegetables are high in "antioxidants" which is fancy for "fighters of disease." They therefore prevent you from getting sick as often, and help fight off diseases such as heart disease, cancer, etc. If you are an athlete, fruits and vegetables help your body recover after a long workout. Oh, and they also help to make you "regular," if you know what we mean.

- *Fats*: Don't forget to add fats! A fat source is recommended at each meal. This could be avocado, hummus, mayo, dressing, a dipping sauce, nuts, or a snack containing fat like a cookie or chocolate. Fats are good for the brain, and are needed to make important hormones in the body like estrogen and testosterone. Both help you to make strong bones and are vital for functions like building strength and getting a period, among other things. And no, fats don't make you fat. Fats that come from food are called "lipids" or dietary fats, and dietary fats don't have the power to cause a person to gain fat any more than any other food group. Fat makes food taste good, and makes food more fun and pleasurable. This makes us more satisfied and likely to stop sooner. Like proteins, fats help to keep you full throughout the day since they take longer to leave your stomach. So, eat the one "real" cookie versus 20 fat-free ones.

- *Dairy*: Consider adding a dairy source such as milk, chocolate milk, or yogurt. Dairy helps make your bones strong. Teens need 3–4 servings of dairy or a dairy equivalent (like soy milk) per day to meet the recommended dietary allowance (RDA) of 1300mg. We only have until our mid-20s to build as much bone density as we can; after that, we are no longer able to build bone. That's why it's important for teens to have as much dairy as they can during this unique window of opportunity.

Breakfast

Begin the day with a great breakfast that is balanced with all the food groups present. Kids often miss breakfast, but there is evidence to suggest that having breakfast each day makes you smarter and more focused, and increases your energy. And here's a cool fact: studies show that those who eat breakfast have a more nutrient-rich diet than those who skip breakfast. This makes sense, because breakfast skippers are more likely to overeat later on, on unplanned foods, because they get too low on the Hunger Meter (see Chapter 7).

Breakfast ideas:

- Oatmeal with almonds and berries, glass of milk

- Cereal and milk, banana slices, with turkey sausage on the side

- Greek yoghurt with granola, fruit sprinkled with cashews

- Pancakes with strawberries and butter, with a smoothie

- Peanut butter on toast with banana slices, glass of milk

- Eggs and toast, avocado slices, pear

Lunch

So, after you've rocked a great a breakfast, let's focus on how to pack a good lunch. Don't forget to include all food groups. Suggestions include:

- Turkey sandwich with cheese and avocado, carrots

- Peanut butter jelly with wheat thins on the side, apple, yogurt

- Pizza, salad with dressing

- Chicken stir-fry over rice, with mandarin oranges

- Pre-packaged salad (chicken Caesar salad) with pita on the side, salad dressing

Afternoon Snack

When you come home from school, what will you eat? We often hear about kids coming home from school feeling ravenous, a 1–2 on the Hunger Meter. If we are right, and you are in fact a 1–2 on the Hunger Meter, the goals here are to aim to move you away from 1–2 on the Hunger Meter towards 3–4 and to be prepared with a plan. This will enable you to eat mindfully, prevent overeating, and enable you to eat the foods you really want, rather than eating whatever you see in front of you. To move you towards 3–4 on the Hunger Meter, let's first figure out why you are so hungry.

1. Did you skip a meal? Come on, 'fess up, did you have time to eat breakfast...?

2. Were your meals too small?

3. Did you forget to bring a morning snack with you?

4. Did your meals have all the food groups represented (carbohydrates like bread or rice, protein like chicken or turkey, fats like avocado or nuts, dairy like milk or yogurt, and a fruit or vegetable)?

5. Were your meals too boring? Were they bland?

6. Or are you eating the same thing every day? Sometimes boring meals will leave you wanting more.

Based on what you determine from the questions above, you will want to make changes in order to get your hunger level up to a 3–4. So, for example, if you missed breakfast, that's an easy one, let's try adding in breakfast. (Yes, you might actually have to wake up 10 minutes earlier.) You can try bringing a morning snack (in between breakfast and lunch) or adding a few items onto your lunch.

It's also good to brainstorm in advance as to what this mid-afternoon snack will be. Plan out some ideas ahead of time. Discuss it with your parents so you have the food items available in the house. Some great ideas at this time of day include:

- Hummus and pita chips

- Cookies and milk

- Granola bar and fruit

- Apple and peanut butter

- Guacamole and tortilla chips

- Banana and almond butter on bread

- Brownie and milk

- Banana bread and an apple

- Yogurt and granola

- Smoothie

- Half of a peanut butter jelly sandwich (or whole depending on your appetite/energy needs)

- Trail mix and milk

- Cashews and dark chocolate

If you are an athlete, your after-school snack will also serve as your pre-workout snack; this is important for fueling your muscles during practice and giving you enough energy to compete. Some athletes go straight to practice after school, missing this important opportunity to fuel. Taking a snack after school, and before practice, will not only help you feel strong on the field, but will also help you maintain more control at dinner after practice.

Otherwise, if you skip that important snack time, you might find you end up overeating after practice when you get home. Ideally you would be a Level 4 here, not starving but ready to have your pre-workout snack. Even if you are starving after school, it is not recommended to eat more than a snack at this time. Eating too much right before going out on the field could cause you to feel nauseous or sluggish. If your hunger hits a Level 2 or 3, it is usually because your lunch was insufficient and that should be increased going forward.

Whether you are an athlete or not, the most important thing is to make sure you that you have what you need, when you are hungry. This may involve having that conversation with Mom and Dad.

Let's say, for example, you're in a time crunch and you run into the house to grab a snack. There is a bag of Halloween candy and the "makings" for a sandwich. The easier choice is the candy since the sandwich isn't made. The candy tastes great but will not give you sustained energy. You're stuck because you don't have the time or maybe the desire to make a sandwich even though you would have been satisfied with one. This is why planning ahead is helpful; otherwise you might down whatever is quickest instead of what your body actually needs.

Dinner

Dinner time is a chance to relax after a long day, catch up with your folks, and eat together as a family. Believe it or not, there is a lot of research out there about the value of eating together as a family. Plating a balanced plate will help you get in all your nutrients, and will feel more satisfying than plating only rice, for example. Consider including proteins such as chicken, beef, salmon, shrimp, pork, tofu, or beans, with starches such as rice, quinoa, couscous, pasta, tortellini, or bread, with a good hearty dose of vegetables such as broccoli, spinach, kale, carrots, asparagus, peppers, cucumbers, salads, mushrooms, or green beans. Suggestions for a complete meal include:

- Chicken with rice, broccoli and a glass of milk

- Taco night: Ground turkey (or vegetarian option with black beans and/or tofu), tortilla, salsa, cheese, avocado with sautéed vegetables

- Roasted chicken with green beans, sweet potatoes and a glass of milk

- Spaghetti and meatballs with parmesan cheese and salad with dressing

- Pizza and salad with dressing

After-Dinner Snack

It's not uncommon to feel hungry a few hours after dinner. If this happens to you, don't forget about an after-dinner snack. For ideas, see the list of snacks on page 92.

True mindful eaters accommodate their authentic appetite by preparing to support its varied tastes with a range of foods that are all equal in availability. Catering to your tastes while you are on the go takes a bit of preliminary work. This may mean having a stash of on-the-go foods in your backpack, your locker, or your car. This is especially important if you are one of those people who finds yourself overriding your hunger because you are waiting until you get home to your food. If you are going to commit to listening for your body's hunger signals, then it's essential to be prepared to respond to that signal.

Many of us feel we never have time to eat. When we do eat, we grab whatever we can find, which may not match our energy needs. Treat yourself like you matter enough to take the time each day to have a quiet lunch. This will be especially important when learning to get back to what your body already knows how to do: eat in response to your first signal of hunger, honor your body's cravings, and stop at just enough.

Get back into the habit of packing the foods you know you love on a regular basis or asking your parents to help you pack them. Help your parents with cooking and try to discover new foods. Pick out a recipe that looks fun, get involved in chopping vegetables, and mixing the food ingredients, and learning how to cook! Use the time prepping and chopping and preparing your food as an opportunity to practice mindfulness. It will feel good to spend the time preparing your food in a way that makes it equal in availability. With all foods accessible and equally easy to grab, you can reach for what your body's calling for and enjoy it.

Chapter 7

The Hunger Meter

Learning Our Body's Language

Connected eating is simple, but it's not easy. Before we delve into connected eating, we want to make sure that we're speaking the same language—specifically with regard to what it means to be hungry and what it means to be full. Although we're hopeful that this section will teach you how to recognize when you are hungry and when you are full, there may be a fair amount of confusion to start. But we promise you this: if you are patient and willing to experiment, you're likely to discover better ways to understand your own appetite. This will help you know when to have more and when you have had enough. We are going to accomplish this by introducing you to a new tool, the Hunger Meter.

Think of this chapter as similar to watching a well-crafted thriller. Early on, you're sure you've missed some crucial piece of information that will prevent you from following the movie through to the end, but it always comes full circle. It's no different with your food. Trust that with time and practice you'll fully understand the different levels of hunger and satiation.

The Hunger Meter: From Ravenous to Just Right

Try using a simple meter as an image to understand the varying stages of appetite, from hunger to satiety. When you first get your driver's permit, you'll keep your eye on the speedometer to make sure you aren't driving too fast or too slow—same thing you'll want to do with the Hunger Meter. If you go too slow, you'll start to lose speed; start eating too early, you're pushing the pedal to the metal when it's not necessary. The goal is to land right in the middle: not holding up traffic, or, conversely, finding yourself in traffic school for the weekend. The goal is to use just the right amount of gas, while at the same time knowing when to put the brakes on.

Starting Places

Level 1

Usually at this level you're starving. You may feel dizzy, or extremely cranky. Your brain, depleted of fuel, may cause you to feel like it can't think clearly. You may feel weak and fatigued.

It might be hard to focus on what you are reading. Remember the last time you skipped a meal because you had to study or something really important came up? Remember how suddenly and fiercely hungry you felt after things settled down? This could set you up to be ravenous enough to eat someone, like your friend, which would be a little rough on the rapport.

When here, you'll have difficulty stopping at "just enough." Eating in this zone of the meter can have a rapid, almost out-of-your-mind quality to it. So it's easy to miss the right stopping place.

There can also be an obsessive quality that comes with this level. Let's say you reach a Level 1 while you are finishing up a meeting that you have to go to at school. You're at Level 1 with your hunger but there is no food around. Your mind may think about food over and over again in an obsessive way. It will go something like this: "I'm hungry." Two minutes pass. "I wonder if Avery has some food in her backpack?" One minute passes. "John is eating something there. Wonder if he would mind if I had some?" Thirty seconds pass. "Maybe I have food in my locker." One minute passes. "I could say I have to go to the bathroom and run to my locker quickly...?" Meanwhile, you just missed the last 10 minutes of what was going on in your meeting and all you're thinking about is how to get your hands on some food. Extreme hunger can be very distracting.

When you're under-fueled and hungry, your blood sugar drops low. This signals the body to begin to break down muscle for fuel. Breaking down muscle gives the body some fuel, which may cause you to feel less hungry. But this is not the preferred way, of course—muscle is kinda cool, we're assuming you'd like to keep it.

At this stage, it's not uncommon for people to say: "I'm not really hungry anymore." Uh, yes, you are. You've just let your hunger go underground, like being exhausted and getting a second wind.

Level 2

At Level 2, you have slightly more control than at Level 1. You may not have as many physiological symptoms such as dizziness or fatigue, and your brain may be a little sharper. But you are still very hungry. Your stomach may be rumbling loudly and you may be getting some weird looks from people nearby.

Similar to Level 1, you will also be at risk for overeating. The intensity of the hunger may propel you to take more food than what your body really needs, or eat so quickly that you bypass your brain's ability to recognize that it's full. It takes the brain some time to catch up to the stomach and register that you are full, usually 20 minutes or so. Food needs to be broken down or digested. This is a complex system but the end goal is to take the important nutrients from your food and ship them over to the parts of your body that need them (calcium to your bones, for example).

This pathway of complex signals and deliveries happens quickly but not instantly. Thus, your brain doesn't know that you are full right away. This is why eating regularly and slowly is important so that you don't overdo it when you are starving, and then end up stuffed and uncomfortable.

Level 3

Ahhh, now we're arriving at a manageable hunger. You feel calm and mindful about the decision to eat. You're not ravenous, but you may feel a little twinge in your stomach, a little emptiness telling you that your body wants food. You know it's been a while since you had your last meal, and you feel ready to find food so your brain and body can perform at an optimum level. There is less drama here. You're not obsessing about food, your brain is functioning well, and your body feels healthy. But it's time to eat, and you can calmly figure out, hungry for what? To determine what it is you actually want to eat, tune in and decide from the inside what *taste*, *texture*, and *temperature* you'd like your food choice to be. (More on what we call the 3 Ts in Chapter 8.)

Level 4

This is the gray zone and harder to describe. You might not have many physical cues telling you that you are hungry but you probably "could" eat. If lunch is at 12, and you have a break for a snack at 2pm, you might find that you are a "4" on the Hunger Meter at this time. You could eat, but you're not that hungry. At Level 4, you may also feel snacky. If something's really tempting, like the fries when you're hanging out with your friends, you might say yes, but you might also say no.

Level 5

You've probably just eaten, and aren't hungry. At this point, your pull toward food is likely emotional not physical. You might ask yourself, "If it wasn't about the food, what would it be about?" The whole point of an emotion is to signal you that there's a need. If you hang out with an emotion long enough, you might, for example, identify a feeling of boredom. Do your best not to feed boredom, instead, pay attention to different ideas of things to do for entertainment. Does the idea of going to the movies tire you or inspire you? Journaling? Hanging out with a friend? Are you craving solitude or socialization? It's good to have a list available of fun activities to do when you get into this zone, otherwise, you might reach for food even when you're not hungry. (Check out Chapter 11, on foodless fulfillment, for a list of ideas for how to keep busy.)

Stopping Places

Level 6

Another ahhh! This is the dreamy stopping place. Don't worry, you can eat again when you get hungry; it's not like this is your last chance. Your stomach feels happy and at peace, it's not overly stuffed and not looking for more. Your future self will totally dig that you were able to stop at just enough.

Level 7

You've passed level 6. This is not a bad space to be in, especially if this becomes your new "full" (versus levels 8 to 10). Fun fact: our taste buds lose interest much beyond this point. Just another cool thing the body does to let us know we're at a nice stopping place.

Level 8

You are on the path toward full, feeling anchored by your food. You might not like this feeling if "bow pose" is in your near future, but otherwise, no big deal. (Bow pose is a yoga pose where you lay face down on your mat, then bend the back into the shape of an archer's bow.)

Level 9

This is Thanksgiving Dinner full. You are uncomfortable here, and you're feeling like you just want to go and sit on the couch and not do much. Though you're fueled, you're not feeling particularly energized, you ate past the point of energy and you probably just want to nap. If your goal is to eat in a way that feels good during and after your meal, you're straying off that path.

Level 10

Uh oh. Time to unbutton. Your short-term decision to eat beyond fullness has made you feel miserable. Now you feel like the friend you could have eaten at Level 1 is sitting on you.

What Is Your Current Relationship to Hunger?

While you're at school, you might consistently override your hunger (intentionally or unintentionally) and wind up in the Level 1 or 2 zone when you get home. When you are at home on a Sunday, you might feed boredom at Level 4 or 5, and keep yourself there all day. You never let yourself really get hungry.

Turning the light onto food behaviors that were previously in the dark will give you the chance to actually do something about them. Being awake and aware of your current relationship to hunger is a critical step to changing it. But you also need to keep in mind that this relationship is constantly changing. So, figure out the lay of the land right here and now, but be sure to check in often because the landscape is certain to change.

When you start paying attention to your food habits you might start to recognize that you let yourself get to extremes that are not working for you. It's the same thing as waiting until the last minute to finish that essay or project that's due on Monday. Cramming just exhausts you, and may lead to you writing a paper that isn't the quality that you were aiming for.

The better you understand what you need and the more you plan ahead, the more manageable it is. The same thing applies to food. Learning about your unique Hunger Meter helps you to manage your needs and eat and enjoy everything in a way that works for you.

Chapter 8

Eating with Manageable Hunger

In Chapter 7 we spent some time defining the different stages of hunger. We noted that, although we have various emotional drivers toward food, it is real hunger at Level 3 that signals if our body is truly ready to eat. In Chapter 3, we discussed the importance of quieting our mind so we can clearly hear our body speaking to us. Knowing what real hunger is and listening for hunger is a great start. But don't be surprised if it takes more.

Whether you're a person who has habitually done what Geneen Roth calls "eating for hunger to come" (lurking at Levels 4 or 5 on the Hunger Meter) or you're one of those expert overriders who regularly denies being hungry or actively suppresses it (a Level 1 or 2 inhabitant) chances are, it is going to take some work for you and your appetite to reconnect. But like peanut butter and jelly, they are destined to join forces.

Get to know your real appetite like it's your BFF, 'cause it will be. Hunger is based in the science of your body. Think about it, it's a survival response because food is fuel (you're going to see that message a lot). When the body is low on fuel, the brain gets a message from different parts of your body, including your stomach. A hunger signal is a clear signal that it's time to eat. Targeting a "3" on the Hunger Meter will enable you to take a breath and be peaceful about your food selection. And by being hungry, but not starving, you will be better equipped to stop eating without overshooting. When you start with manageable hunger, it will also make it easier to recognize a good stopping point—the goal is to "3 to 6 it." Now is also the time to bust out those 3 Ts. What taste, texture, and temperature do you want to enjoy in this go around? Sidenote: it may sound redundant, but you can only read your hunger when you are actually hungry, this doesn't work at a 4+ on the Hunger Meter, 'cause you're not hungry.

You probably don't want hot soup on a hot summer day or a popsicle right after skiing. Maybe you do and that's okay too. The point is, taking a minute to clue into what your body is craving will help you make a more satisfying choice.

TOM ON MANAGEABLE HUNGER: 15 YEARS OLD

Tom loves In-N-Out Burger. He and his friends like to stop there after lacrosse practice. In session, Tom said that he notices that if he forgets to eat before practice he gets to a "2" on the Hunger Meter, orders a "double double," large fries, and a large milkshake. His eyes become bigger than his stomach.

Starting at a "2" inevitably means he lands at a 9+ on the Hunger Meter every time, uncomfortably full when he's finished. Whereas if he eats a good lunch and a pre-workout snack, his pattern is that he'll be a "3" when he goes to order. Here, he reports being able to tune in and peacefully decide, from the inside, what he wants to eat. He's practicing using the 3 Ts for taste, texture, temperature he'd like his food selection to be. Sometimes, on a hot day, he might only get a shake, another day maybe only a burger, and occasionally a "double double" with fries. At a "3" he has manageable hunger, and doesn't need to try very hard to determine what he wants to eat or when to stop.

Your appetite may not be a morning person. Not all of us are. To keep your body's metabolism on track, you should be diving into that initial meal within the first hour of getting up. If you are new to this process, you will want to keep your metabolism firing by eating regularly throughout the day. Eating every 3–4 hours is a good way to teach yourself to feel hungry throughout the day, while preventing you from feeling ravenous later on.

For example, you wake up at 7am. Perhaps breakfast is at 7:30am. Depending on what time your lunch is, you might need a snack mid-morning at 9:30–10 when your belly starts rumbling. Aim for lunch by 12, snack at 3pm after school, dinner at 6, and an evening snack at 9. If it's a weekend, and you sleep in, no worries. If you're up at 11am that morning, everything just gets shifted. Breakfast would be at 11, lunch at 2pm, snack at 4 or 5, dinner at 8, and snack at 10 or 11.

As you get more comfortable with this, you can eventually transition to eating in response to your body's hunger cues. When you get hungry will depend on when, what, and how much you last ate—which seems incredibly obvious, but if you're used to loitering mindlessly on the Hunger Meter all day, this will actually take considerable listening skills.

BROOKE ON DISCOVERING HER HUNGER: 16 YEARS OLD

Brooke writes: While I was in my last stages of healing my disconnected eating, I finally got the green light from my registered dietitian to start connected eating. When I heard this, I thought it was going to be a cakewalk compared to what I had been going through. Then I started to realize I had no idea where to begin with eating to appetite because I hadn't had hunger in such a long time. I thought that to be hungry my stomach had to be in knots and I had to hear dying whale sounds. After a while I began to realize hunger was a much less obvious cue. For example, I found that every few hours I would have a thought pop into my head of something that sounded tasty, and with some further analyzing, I would register this thought as a real craving for food.

We keep mentioning food as "fuel" for the body. Well, let's just use that word to discuss metabolism. Have you seen those cartoons with the old-school steam engine trains? The crazed train robber shovels batches of coal into the fire to make it burn hotter and hotter, making the engine run faster and faster. You get where we are going with this. A well-fueled metabolism is a hot burning fire that will digest and support how well your body functions. If you don't get enough coal/fuel in the engine, the train stops.

But here's another important piece to this metaphor. After a point, the engine can't burn any more fuel. Extra coal just won't do anything more and doesn't actually do anything to enhance the furnace (actually they called it a firebox). So, you need fuel to keep the fire going and you need enough to make things work optimally. Think about a well-conditioned athlete. If they don't eat well before a race, they are going to run out of steam and not perform at their best. Interestingly enough, that's where the idiom "running out of steam" comes from. It comes from old steam engines that didn't have enough fuel to keep going.

READING THE HUNGER METER

Did we mention how challenging it can be to hear your body's "voice" if you've become accustomed to listening only to your head? This short exercise is great to use before and after meals for the first few weeks of committing to reconnecting with your body's wisdom. After that, use it for those times where you might be confused, and we know that happens.

So, where are you on the meter of 1 to 10 right now?

_____

How do you know?

_____
_____
_____
_____
_____
_____
_____
_____
_____
_____
_____
_____
_____
_____
_____
_____
_____

Discovering Your 3 Ts

The 3 Ts (taste, texture, and temperature) work best if your hunger is at a manageable place on the Hunger Meter, not too hungry. When you get the first inkling that you are hungry, tune in and decide from the inside what it is you'd like to eat this go-around.

- Taste: are you looking for something salty like pretzels? Sweet like chocolate? Or savory like cheese?

- Temperature: do you want something cold and refreshing like watermelon? Or warm and soothing like soup?

- Texture: are you looking for some crunchy like chips? Chewy like dried fruit? Or soft like yogurt or ice cream?

DISCOVERING YOUR 3 TS

Tune in and decide from the inside what it is you'd like to eat now:

Taste? _____
_____
_____
_____

Temperature? _____
_____
_____
_____

Texture? _____
_____
_____
_____

Taste? _____
_____
_____
_____

Temperature? _____
_____
_____
_____

Texture? _____
_____
_____
_____

EATING IN A WAY THAT HONORS YOUR FUTURE SELF

There is a big difference between demonizing food and knowing which foods are best for certain situations. For instance, brownies are the perfect choice when your 3 Ts are sweet, chewy, and warm. But if you have soccer practice on the horizon, you might want to consider something a little more substantial that contains not only carbohydrates but also some protein, like a smoothie, Greek yogurt, or a bag of trail mix. You can still have the brownie of course, but perhaps save it for after the workout. Otherwise, you might find that your stomach is rumbling during your workout or you might run out of steam before practice ends. And just to add, there will of course be people who love brownies pre-workout, so this is all individual and can require some trial and error.

Combined with the 3 Ts, the following questions will help you to quickly check in with yourself and your schedule for that day:

Where are you on the Hunger meter?

_____

_____

_____

_____

_____

_____

_____

_____

_____

_____

What will you be doing later today?

_____
_____
_____
_____
_____
_____
_____
_____
_____
_____

What type of food do you think will be a good choice given this kind of activity?

_____
_____
_____
_____
_____
_____
_____
_____
_____
_____

Chapter 9

All Foods Are Fair Game

Okay. Now that you have befriended your appetite, it's time to take the "boo" out of what many people consider to be frightening foods.

You know what we're talking about here. Many of us feel like we'd be fine if we just didn't have any of those pink pastry boxes anywhere around us. Not possible. The whole I'll-eat-it-if-it's-there-so-am-banking-on-not-having-access-to-it approach is pretty much not sustainable. Letting your environment choose your food (meaning your environment is making decisions rather than you) doesn't allow you to develop self-trust or act on your body's real appetite. This shuts down your listening skills. Don't let food run the show. A donut isn't the boss of you. It's just a donut.

Free yourself from its tyranny. That happens by learning how to listen to yourself and paying attention to your wants and needs. That need could very well be a donut and that's okay. It could also not be a donut and that's okay too. All foods can be part of a healthy diet, even donuts.

JOHNIE ON CHILDHOOD MEMORIES OF HER "HEALTHY" HOUSEHOLD: 25 YEARS OLD

My story about "bad" foods is like many I've heard. It started as far back as I can remember. In one of my households, my parents' strategy was to have only "healthy" food in the house. We were "that" Halloween house that handed out walnuts or toothbrushes and always had a plethora of nonfat milk, turkey bacon, tofu, and carob-coated raisins.

I try my best to forget those elementary school lunches where I'd stare longingly at other kids' lunchboxes stuffed with sandwiches made with Wonder Bread, Twinkies, and cartons of whole milk. When I couldn't take it anymore, I'd try to get salesy with them—proposing a trade of my fig bars for their Doritos. I was desperate to ditch the fig bars. Not the dreamy ones with the jam in the middle, the ones from the health food store that looked like they were ready to sprout. I'd even offer to throw in my carob-coated raisins. No go, every time.

As I got older and had more access to food outside of my household, I recall watching in amazement as my childhood friend, whose household was far less restrictive than mine, seemed to "decide from the inside" and eat mostly with hunger. She'd often choose nutritionally dense foods even when she had full access to the Ho Hos drawer, Coca Cola, and leftover pizza. While she would casually grab a snack—I would raid her pantry with or without actual physical hunger, not knowing when I'd have access to these "off limits" foods again.

A lot has changed since then, and now I have total food freedom (R.I.P. carob-coated raisins).

Here's the deal: avoiding a food item makes you want it more. Avoidance creates a certain desire for the food and reinforces a fear of it. Being fearful of foods limits your freedom and fun.

You may struggle to eat at a friend's house, to eat in college cafeterias or on a road trip. Fearful eating, or rigid eating, puts you more at risk for binging. The more you avoid something, the more the temptation for it builds. The key is learning to listen to yourself and being okay with the choice.

To master listening to your body, you will need to really let go of your preconceived feelings around food. Intellectually avoiding things all the time "because you are supposed to" or "should" makes you like a walking time bomb, waiting to have a caloric explosion. If you walk into a coffee shop, see a piece of chocolate cake that looks good to you, but then tell yourself, "No, I can't have a piece, I am trying to look good for prom," it's like telling yourself to not think about purple elephants. Go ahead, try it. For the next 60 seconds, don't think about purple elephants. Think about anything else...time yourself, 60 seconds on the clock.

How'd that go?

Telling yourself you can't have something is likely to activate your inner rebel, which is cool for other things (like asserting yourself, having boundaries, and speaking your truth...), but activate that part of ourselves around food and we're likely to end up eating a whole cake.

Connected eaters allow themselves to eat cake when they want it. That choice takes the air out of being scared because then cake is just cake. Sometimes they might even say no to having cake because it's not their favorite kind. If they had a piece, they would know when to stop. This helps to create a long-term sustainable relationship with food.

It's not uncommon to feel like if you allowed yourself to have foods you considered "bad," that's all you would eat. Imagine if we asked you to eat cookies for dessert every day for 30 consecutive days. On day 31, if we offered you a cookie, your stomach might turn at the very thought of it. Including a variety of different foods helps to neutralize food, with no one food being more enticing than others. Practicing this over and over again, helps to obliterate this idea of "good foods and bad foods" from your mind. If you can and do eat everything, it takes the power out of food, and you can experience food freedom.

COY ON FAST FOOD: 13 YEARS OLD

Coy refused to eat at a fast food restaurant on the way home from their football game. "I would rather not eat than have fast food," they said at the time. But it was 4 hours later when they were able to eat at home. It is important to eat right away after a workout, to optimize how the body recovers, get reenergized for the next day, and reduce inflammation. By delaying when they ate, they missed refueling during that crucial recovery window 1-2 hours post-workout, which arguably would harm them more than having fast food. Most sports nutritionists would likely agree that, given the choice between eating fast food or skipping the post-workout meal and eating nothing, it is better for you to eat fast food post-workout.

To be "free," there would also need to be the elimination of food rules, most of which are arbitrary and without scientific merit. For example, you may have heard that it is not good to eat after a certain time at night. One article may say "don't eat after 7" and a different one might say "don't eat after 9." So, which is it?

Neither, actually, unless you have a medical condition like reflux. There is no scientific evidence to support that eating after a certain time causes weight gain. In fact, eating a snack is a good idea to give your body fuel while you are sleeping. This may sound odd, why would your sleeping body need fuel? Well, the body is quite busy at night, growing, repairing muscles, and integrating new information and skills into memory. If you ate dinner at 6pm, and didn't eat afterward, and if you woke up the next morning at 6am, your body wouldn't have had fuel for 12 hours! Eating before bed can minimize that effect. A night snack is especially important for athletes training after school, and becomes an important part of the body's recovery process.

Treating all food with fairness and debunking diet myths, like those stated above, keeps the focus on eating in response to your body's wisdom. Besides, classifying foods as inherently good or bad is not necessary. Now if you go hit your friend on the head with a stale baguette, and it hurts them, well that's bad. But eating one? C'mon.

Instead of saying no to certain foods, and making yourself want them all the more, you can decide experientially if the food jives with you. For example, let's say, Pop-Tarts might be available for breakfast and instead of saying, "Pop-Tarts are bad and I shouldn't eat them or my teeth will rot and my insides will fall out," you follow your craving. But make your decision to have Pop-Tarts for breakfast not only by how it tastes initially—but also by the way it feels in your body afterward. That way the decision is made not by forbidding the food but instead by saying, "I can have a Pop-Tart anytime I want, yet it's probably not going to be my breakfast choice when I have the SATs in the morning."

Legalizing all foods takes the power out of foods that you might consider to be "bad." Stop hating on chips and ice cream—these foods by themselves are not what leads someone to overshoot their body's natural weight. Work on separating foods from good and bad categories; that way the foods that you're genuinely craving will satisfy you physically and emotionally. This will also prevent you from overly reacting to foods you don't let yourself have.

When our food choices spring from fear—when we become fearful about anything, for that matter—we release cortisol in our bodies. It makes you wonder which is worse for our health, the nutritionally challenged food or the worry about the food. Fear is stress. Reminder from Chapter 3, that sometimes stress is good in that it motivates you to get that book report done, but a lot of other times it's not good and can be hard on your system.

Think about the last time you got scared. Do you remember if your heart started to beat faster? Did you feel your cheeks flush? Well, although unpleasant, that's all very normal. That's the stress response. No, you aren't necessarily feeling that when you are thinking about having that piece of cake you don't think you should have, but your body may be experiencing that on a smaller scale.

The point is, making decisions from fear leads to unhealthy effects not just because of the emotional toll but also because of the physical toll. This physical toll doesn't help digestion, it doesn't help energy levels, and it can decrease how efficiently your body metabolizes food. It's not just the food that you eat that makes you healthy. It's also the way you feel about those choices. This is why we want you to eat and enjoy everything in a way that works for you. Our big point here is that making conscious choices that are based on what you want and need can promote good health in general.

Why We Eat What We Eat

Lucy Aphramor's "Why We Eat What We Eat" activity reflects her Well Now approach. As Lucy says, "the current trend of choosing foods based mainly on nutrients discounts our likes and dislikes, tastes, cravings, values, etc. It disconnects us from our body signals, from social occasion and ignores our circumstances. In this way, it teaches a diet mentality way of relating to food."[1]

The Well Now approach teaches that food and eating serve many roles and meet a range of needs and desires around health, pleasure, identity, values, family, social, and emotional aspects of life. Nutrients are an important part of the picture, but not the only part. There is a lot more to food and eating than vitamins, sugars, and fiber! Recognizing this can help us feel more relaxed around food and better able to eat in ways that nourish ourselves physically, mentally, socially, and so on.

This activity looks at why we eat what we eat to keep all aspects of food, eating, and nutrition in perspective.

What you will need: paper plate, pens, and colored pens.

CONNOR ON "WHY WE EAT WHAT WE EAT": 16 YEARS OLD

Why do you choose one type of apple over another type of apple?

mostly I'd choose the apple based on what my parents got from the grocery store. They really like Fuji apples, so that's what we usually have, but if I asked them for a different type of apple they'd get it for me.

Why do you choose particular foods on specified days of the week, month, or year?

Well, definitely one thing I really like is eggnog. So, when it starts showing up in the store, I start asking my parents to get me some. I probably have like a glass everyday or every other day when it's in season. I go through it pretty quickly.

(How) does what you feel influence what you eat?

How I feel might not influence what I eat but how much I eat. If I was feeling down I might not eat as much 'cause I'd just want to go back into my room. But if I'm feeling good I might ask my mom or dad if they want to go out and grab an ice cream after dinner.

Are there foods you avoid? If so, why is this?

I would avoid fish because I don't like the taste. I don't dislike red meat but if I had a choice I'd rather eat chicken. I find red meat tough, whereas chicken is nice and moist and it doesn't hurt my jaw. And there are so many different ways you can cook chicken, like you can have spicy buffalo wings or tangy chicken piccata... I feel like chicken is the superior meat.

Now, ask yourself "Why We Eat What We Eat" and draw, or write, the answers on your plate or on the next page.

WHY WE EAT WHAT WE EAT[2]

Why do you choose one type of apple over another type of apple?

_____

_____

_____

Why do you choose particular foods on specified days of the week, month, or year?

_____

_____

_____

(How) does what you feel influence what you eat?

_____

_____

_____

Are there foods you avoid? If so, why is this?

_____

_____

_____

What themes emerge? If you choose to do this with someone else, it can be fun to pool your answers and group them into categories. eg. practical issues, social and cultural reasons, values, pleasure, identity, well-being and so on.

What have you learned from this activity?

_____

_____

_____

Which Foods Press Your Buttons?

The diet trends in our culture, which are often very restrictive and not designed for teens, have left many people scared to eat freely. Building up your core sense of comfort with foods will make you less dependent on external conditions, such as always needing to have "healthy" foods around. Instead of quitting certain food groups, we'd recommend working on creating a healthy relationship with them.

Are there foods that you find yourself avoiding? For example, do you try to stay away from cookies? Or ice cream? How strong is this avoidance? Which fear foods would be on your list? Julie, a client of ours, noticed she was avoiding several foods. She absolutely wouldn't touch candy of any sort, and would definitely not eat pizza because she was afraid it was too oily. She also thought cookies and cake weren't great, so stayed away from those too. Julie acquired her hesitancy around foods containing sugar through something she read in a magazine.

It's important to examine where your concerns are coming from. For example, sugar can get a bad rap, but it provides energy, and makes food more pleasurable and satisfying by improving taste and texture. Sometimes we crave sugar if we are overly hungry (1–2 on the Hunger Meter) since it gives us quick energy, sometimes it's simply a craving without hunger. Eating regularly throughout the day, as explained in Chapter 6, will help you to curb cravings and eat with a more manageable hunger.

Registered dietitian Marsha Hudnall says, "Forbidden fruit tastes the sweetest. If you really want to ramp up your sweet tooth, tell yourself you shouldn't eat sugar. You'll likely become obsessed with it."[3] Julie realized her fear of foods containing sugar was unfounded. When she allowed herself to start eating them again, nothing bad happened. And a cookie returned to just being a cookie again.

To begin the journey of dissolving your fears around food, you will need to be brave. We will ask you to pick a food (or foods) you've become scared of—maybe from information you may have heard from a friend or read in a magazine, or for no reason—and to eat it! The goal of this exercise is not to get rid of the foods pressing your buttons, but instead to dissolve your buttons. To determine which food(s) to choose first, you might want to make a list of all the foods that press your buttons, and then rank them on a scale of 1–10, with 10 being the most scary and 1 being the least scary. Here is Julie's list.

**Julie's List, Ranked on a Scale of 1–10
(10 = most feared; 1 = least feared)**

Pizza _____9

Ice cream _____6

Cookies_____7

Candy _____8

Chocolate _____7

Then, teach your fear a lesson by heading toward it in order to dissolve the fear. Pack some of this food for lunch or have it at dinner or go enjoy it at a restaurant. It can take several exposures to this scary food (research says like 15–20 times[4]) before it begins to feel neutral. Repeated exposures of the feared food will help convert the food eventually into "no big deal." Otherwise, the avoidance of the scary food will ensure the food will always stay scary.

Try eating the food you chose above or near a Level 3 on the Hunger Meter to get ultimate satisfaction, allowing yourself to eat it with pleasure, and stop at just enough. Remind yourself, "All is good, I don't need this fear around food." In other words, your fear of a particular food is likely greater than the harm it could actually cause.

For example, if you love pie, but you think you might overeat it if there was a whole pie in the house, go out and have a slice of your favorite kind or bring one slice into the house. Give yourself permission to eat it and savor it. The goal here is to reclaim the power you've been giving to a piece of pie. Initially, you might want to eat pie often, but once you truly believe you can have it anytime you want, your psychological craving for it will diminish, and you will start to develop self-trust. You might also notice that you become increasingly picky about which pie you will eat, since you can now have it anytime you'd like.

Make your own list on the blank lines below of the all foods that make you feel even slightly scared. Use the scale from the client sample above to rank the strength of avoidance from 1-10 (1 being not very strong and 10 being extremely strong) for each food.

Ask yourself how you acquired hesitancy around this particular food or food group? And be honest with yourself about whether or not that hesitancy is really warranted.

WHICH FOODS PRESS YOUR BUTTONS?

- _____
- _____
- _____
- _____
- _____
- _____
- _____
- _____
- _____
- _____
- _____
- _____
- _____
- _____

Food Thought Record

Every time you have a freak-out about eating a certain food that has been off limits in the history of you, let your curiosity surface. Why exactly are you freaking out? What do you think is going to happen if you eat this food? Is that fear based in reality?

The Food Thought Record exercise allows you to understand the fear a bit better: break it down into its parts, stop ruminating, and return to baseline more quickly. Remember that book report that was due? It wasn't just the report that was stressing you out, it was also the time crunch.

When you can more clearly understand why you're triggered, it can give you a little more distance from the situation and move you toward a better solution. For example, if you're writing a report, planning the rest of your time in such a way that you complete certain report sections by a certain time will help finishing the report feel more achievable.

By knowing that you're worried that you might eat a churro every time you have access to one at the theme park, you can make an active choice to have one churro, enjoy it, and then give yourself permission to move on with your day.

Use the client example below to prompt ideas for how the Food Thought Records can be filled out. Then go to the blank template and practice filling out your own. Also note that even though these are samples related to food, you can use this skill for any topic at all—it can be more helpful than simply trying to "think" your way out of worry thoughts.

Experience: We are at an amusement park and running from ride to ride. Everyone is having a great time and my friends keep buying caramel corn or candy or churros.

Primary emotion: Fear

Scale 1–100%: 70%

Automatic thought (worst-case scenario):

- I know I'm not hungry but I'm also not stuffed so I keep sharing whenever someone offers.

- I hear about these things not being "healthy" and I'm worried I'm going to gain weight from today.

Evidence to support automatic thought: Caramel corn, candy, and churros are so fattening.

Evidence NOT to support auto thought and to adopt more balanced thought:

- I realize I might eat emotionally occasionally, it's regular emotional eating that is problematic.

- There is not one food, meal, or nutrient associated with poor health or weight gain.

- Normal eating means going with the flow and having fun with food.

- Besides, every meal is a new opportunity to get a little closer to my 3 Ts as well as my starting/ stopping places.

- No big deal.

FOOD THOUGHT RECORD

Experience: _____

Primary emotion: _____

Scale 1–100%: _____

Automatic thought (worst-case scenario):

_____

_____

_____

_____

_____

_____

_____

Evidence to support automatic thought:

_____

_____

_____

_____

_____

_____

_____

Evidence NOT to support auto thought and to adopt more balanced thought:

_____

_____

_____

_____

_____

_____

Chapter 10

Stopping at Just Enough

Most people find stopping at just enough is the most difficult guideline for connected eating. Although food tastes so yummy, once you start eating beyond satisfied, your taste buds start to become de-synthesized (or, toned down). There's only momentary satisfaction at best whenever eating beyond your body's real fullness (Levels 8 to 10 on the Hunger Meter).

Stopping at just enough has many parts. Not only is it ideal to start at a "3" on the Hunger Meter (in other words you can't start at your stopping place) so you can read your hunger, you have to also be satisfied emotionally and physically about your choice, and it needs to be equal in availability.

If you're eating emotionally or just because (for reasons other than hunger), you probably won't be satisfied by what you eat and you may realize that you're filling another kind of need like boredom, "I have nothing else to do, so why not eat?" Consider the mantra: you can't ever get enough of what you don't actually need in the first place. So, if you're bored, go do something fun. Otherwise, it's back to playing whack-a-mole, where the mole, AKA your emotion, pops up and you try clubbing it down with the hammer of food. In case you aren't familiar with this game, no matter how many times you whack those moles, they just keep popping up over and over again. Ultimately, you've gotta learn to love the moles and ask them what they need.

Keep up the practice of figuring out exactly what it is you want to eat, and eat that food. For you to be truly satisfied and capable of stopping at "just enough," you have to grant your body what it is craving. Trust your body's wisdom. Once you've figured out what you want to eat, simply eat it. Don't talk yourself out of it and into something else. This is why having different foods that you like around is important. It's not about avoiding food, but eating and enjoying it, and learning how to stop and move on when you are satisfied. Remind yourself that there's more where that came from. You can eat more of that particular food again when you're hungry, we promise, it's not your last chance.

As you get more skilled at honoring your body and eating what you are craving, you will start to notice a more peaceful relationship with food. Your trust in your body's intelligence will grow. Without that skill, nearly everyone is more likely to eat a whole lot more than necessary. As you can see, the guidelines are circular. Stopping at just enough means eating with hunger, as well as reading and responding to your hunger craving on an emotional and physical level.

For example, if you want a piece of pizza but you have a Kind Bar instead, you will be satisfied physically, but not emotionally. Making the effort to choose the food you desire up front, can prevent you from "doubling up." Think of being in a time crunch to buy a dress for a formal. You end up buying a dress you like "okay," your 80 percent dress. After the formal is over, you're out shopping and you see a dress you love, your 100 percent dress, you end up buying that one too. Get it? You just spent twice as much.

When struck with the temptation to eat beyond what your body is asking for, pay attention. Prepare yourself to make it over this hump when it presents itself. It's an important sign. When you're a newbie with this practice, the ability to stop at satisfied (Level 6ish) is a skill that has to be relearned. After all, you did it as a child/toddler; you just don't remember.

Reminder that we are not aiming for always stopping at a "6," it's normal to overeat at times, it's when it becomes a habit/chronic that it's a problem.

As you practice you will notice that overeating will be spaced out more than when you started, and you probably won't overeat as much. What's cool is that once you learn how to do this it becomes a part of your day and you don't have to think too much about it. So, you get better at knowing when you're eating because you're hungry or because you're bored, stressed, distracted, fear-of-missing-out (food FOMO), or basically other reasons that have nothing to do with hunger. This will enable you to create some space between you and the action of eating without appetite.

SADIE'S FOOD FOMO: 13 YEARS OLD

Tonight at dinner with my family, I didn't do that well with food. I was at 9 on the Hunger meter after I was done. We had Chinese food which I ate like I was never going to have it again. I should have acknowledged that I have this pattern with Chinese food and identified the triggers ahead of time. But honestly, in the moment it's hard to acknowledge this. I only realized afterwards. With Chinese food, I always go for seconds. In my mind I have thoughts like, "I don't want it to be gone," or "what if someone else wants to get some more?" I worry if there will still be some left for me. Yesterday, my dad took some rice and I felt a bit of resentment toward him for taking rice. I mean, the thought comes for couple of seconds and I don't think about it again. I don't always get to eat Chinese food. I got my favorite Kung pao chicken and I couldn't resist. I used to do this and not be aware of it. Now that I have the awareness, I have a choice. The next time we get Chinese food I'm going to use my mantra, "There's more where that came from, I can eat more again when I get hungry."

I'll Meet You Half-way

The following exercise can help you start hearing what your body is saying about satiation (or fullness). During each meal, check in with yourself to describe how you feel after you are half-way finished. For example, after eating half of a hearty sandwich and a handful of chips, how do you feel physically? How do you feel emotionally? What is your hunger level like? You might write down, "annoyed because I know I'm at a '7' on the Hunger Meter, but it tastes so good I want the second half," or "comfortable for now, I can eat the rest later when I get hungry." The emphasis here is building awareness about why it is you might struggle with stopping at just enough. Consider this formula: Awareness + Action = Change. Focus on the awareness piece first, and the action part of the equation will fall into place. Once you become aware of what you are up to with food, and why, you can't ever lose it, you can take it with you out to pizza, a buffet, on a cruise, and, heck, you could take it to college!

Post-Meal Log

Use the 3 client samples below as a template for how to fill in the Post-Meal Log exercise section. Jotting down your post-meal thoughts diligently in the beginning will help not only in delaying any habit of eating beyond fullness you might have, but also help you to become aware of any triggers that lead may lead to overeating. It's important to always remember that overeating, in and of itself, is not a problem, that's perfectly normal, it's when overeating becomes a habit or a way to regulate emotion on a regular basis that it can become problematic. This will be an exercise you can refer back to when you are further along, but feeling "off path" with your food.

> When I arrived at school there were donuts in class, so I ate one, just because it was there, even though I'd already had breakfast. Next time I'm going to tune in, identify where I am on the Hunger Meter, and if I'm at a 5+, I'll have the donut another time. Now I'm overfull and I feel sluggish in class.

> After dinner, I was at a comfortable stopping place, but noticed my sister was still eating her pasta, so I got up and got seconds. Next time I will keep my eyes on my own plate and focus on my needs.

> I told myself I should eat the power bar instead of the cookie I had been craving, that resulted in eating the power bar *and* the cookie. Next time I will work on being more aware and mindfully eating what I really want, the cookie. If I still want the power bar, I'll have it, but if I don't, then I will save it for later.

POST-MEAL LOG

Post-Meal Log

_____
_____
_____
_____
_____
_____
_____
_____

Post-Meal Log

_____
_____
_____
_____
_____
_____
_____
_____

Body Awareness

Dr. Anita Johnston, author of *Eating in the Light of the Moon*, says body awareness helps us get back in touch with the physical sensations that tell us when to eat and drink, and when to stop eating and drinking. She states that the signals for thirst are less likely to get entangled with emotional hungers and, for that reason, are easier to begin with.

Dr. Johnston developed a simple tool for body awareness. We'll use the example of drinking water (try it with us!).

Next time you begin to feel thirsty, ask yourself, "How do I know I'm thirsty? What is the physical signal that is telling me I am thirsty?" You might be able to recognize a signal such as a dry throat, a dry tongue...

Then ask yourself, "Okay, how do I know when to stop drinking once I've started?" Your mouth may not feel dry any more, you may sense coolness in your throat...what signals tell you to start/stop?[1]

Use the questions on the next page to help recognize your thirst or hunger, whenever you reach for something to drink or eat.

BODY AWARENESS

Thirst

How do I know I'm thirsty?

_____

_____

_____

_____

What is the physical signal that is telling me I am thirsty?

_____

_____

_____

_____

After taking a few sips, ask yourself:

How do I know when to stop drinking once I've started?

_____

_____

_____

_____

What signals tell me to start/stop?

_____

_____

_____

_____

Hunger

What is the physical sensation that is telling me I'm hungry?

_____

_____

_____

_____

Where in my body do I feel the hunger?

_____

_____

_____

_____

After taking a few bites, ask yourself:

Am I still hungry?

_____

_____

_____

_____

How do I know?

_____

_____

_____

_____

What's the physical signal?

_____

_____

_____

_____

Part III

Adding Tools to Your Toolbox

Chapter 11

What to Do When You Want Food, But You're Not Hungry

Don't Fall for the Foodie Call

Foodie calls are those subliminal pulls toward food when you're not yet truly hungry (Level 4 or higher on the Hunger Meter). Managing them is a key part of achieving connected eating. Foodie calls are just your mind's misguided attempt to squelch some non-physical need. The problem with eating as a way to avoid an uncomfortable feeling—whether that feeling is boredom, anxiety, or something in between—is that it has such a shortened state of well-being. Basically, it only works while it's working. The minute you've swallowed that last bite of cake, you're right back to feeling what it was you were trying to avoid—hence the continued overeating. Keep this mantra close by for help: it's impossible to get enough of what you don't actually need in the first place. If you feel a pull toward food and you're at 4+ on the Hunger Meter, you're not hungry for food, you're hungry for something else!

Chapter 2 explained the biology of emotions as well as how they evolve as we get older. This chapter will cover off on the purpose of emotions and how to manage them skillfully. Neuroanatomist Jill Bolt Taylor asserts that it takes less than 90 seconds for an emotion to get triggered, surge chemically through the bloodstream, then get flushed out.[1] It is typically our response to the emotion that prolongs the emotion, so whatever we feel after the 90 seconds is usually a by-product of a self-created story.

The goal of this chapter is to leave you with an understanding of emotions, how to navigate them more efficiently, cultivate emotional wisdom, and reduce disconnected eating. Understanding the purpose of emotions will enable you to have some distance from them (also known as observing self—like watching a movie versus being in it).

One of many reasons diets don't work is that they never address why you are eating without hunger in the first place. Eating without a genuine cue from your body is often a side effect of not being willing to sit with your current emotions. Learning to tackle your feelings instead of tackling your fridge will require loads of practice before it even becomes comfortable. The good news is that every meal is a new opportunity to get a little closer to eating in response to your body's wisdom. If you make a perceived mistake with food, acknowledge it, and quickly put it in the rear-view mirror.

Many people fall into a pattern of feeding their emotions instead of facing them. It's typical for people who eat for reasons other than hunger to claim they don't know what they feel, other than a mind-driven pull toward food. If a person is in the habit of eating in response to a feeling, guess what happens? They accumulate unresolved feelings in addition to being unable to accurately label them. Recognizing such emotions, and labeling them, is critical to being able to manage them.

Emotions are simply nature's way of signaling that something is wrong, or that something needs attending to. The desired change here is to use your emotions wisely. One way to use your emotions wisely is to strengthen your ability to hang out with uncomfortable feelings without pulling in problematic self-soothing that makes the situation worse. The problematic behavior we are talking about in this case is eating without hunger. Most of us are afraid of our feelings and have become very skilled at avoiding them. The truth is that avoidance maintains fear. We then end up having suppressed emotions that, over time, end up playing Jack-in-the-box on us by popping up in intrusive ways. This makes it difficult to be present in our lives at the current moment. And, in this case, it makes it harder to change our relationship to eating.

Given that an average emotion lasts 90 seconds, whatever we feel after that is called a "secondary response to the primary emotion." So, for example, if Sam's primary emotion is "loneliness," she can respond to the loneliness in a couple of different ways. She can identify and label the loneliness and say to herself, "There's a feeling of loneliness in me right now." The loneliness (primary emotion) would still be painful, but by labeling the emotion, and not bringing a mind-generated story in on the feeling (secondary response), she will reduce the intensity and duration of the emotion. She can also use her emotions wisely by pairing the feeling of loneliness with a healing response like, "I'm worthy of belonging, regardless of whether or not my friends have made plans without me."

On the other hand, if she responds to the emotion with one of her "greatest hits" (a story we tell about ourselves often, usually built on a faulty premise) by saying something like, "Everyone is posting pictures on Instagram of something fun they are doing together this weekend. No one ever invites me, no one likes me," the feeling of loneliness will be prolonged and more intense. Pain is inevitable, suffering is optional. Besides, thoughts are simply neural firings in the brain, not facts of the universe.

There are two types of emotions we are going to focus on here: *recall emotion* and *reality*. The brain is considered by neuroscientists to be a "don't get killed device." It is set up to remember painful experiences on a deep level. So, you might have vague memories of your childhood trips to Disneyland, but your brain can easily recall the details from a time you were teased. When we experience painful events, our brain encodes the emotional memory in our "limbic" brain (also known as emotional brain), whereas positive experiences don't get recorded in the same way. Anytime there is a stimulus in your environment that resembles a time when you were teased, you will likely experience recall emotion—suppressed emotion stored in the emotional brain that has not been discharged. Recall emotion is often more intense than the reality of the situation.

To further illustrate the two different types of emotion, let's say you decide to spend the day with Captain Hook (hang with us here). You decide to go out to a nice lunch, and upon your departure from the restaurant, you both see a gigantic crocodile roaming around outside in the grass. You and Captain Hook will both experience emotions related to the reality of the situation.

You have never encountered a crocodile, but have enough information about them to know that this is probably not good. Captain Hook, on the other hand (pardon the pun), will experience both the reality as well as recall emotion. His brain has recorded the pain of losing his left hand to a crocodile. His emotion will be significantly more intense than yours.

Without the brain's ability to remember painful experiences, Captain Hook would see the crocodile and while scratching his chin trying to remember what it was that he didn't like about crocodiles, CHOMP! He loses his right hand too.

A tool to use when experiencing an emotion of any kind, is to simply ask yourself, "Is this recall or reality?" If you discover that there is recall emotion occurring you can use your emotions wisely by pairing your fear with an affirmation that will help soothe the sympathetic nervous system, such as, "Everything is alright right now. I am safe." This will then be sent down to the emotional brain, healing it just a little more than it was before. These exercises are not transformative, but with continued practice they make a difference.

We hope you are starting to see that one of the keys to regulating emotion is having the ability to allow a feeling to come up, hang out with it long enough to identify it and label it accurately, and respond to it in a way that cultivates freedom. You are not the feeling you are having. Since the brain also makes the strongest connections between things that happen close together in time, it is likely that, if you have a history of chronic emotional eating, anytime an emotion pops up, your brain will likely create an urge to eat (without hunger). It will take habit reversal to wither away this groove in the brain, but, on a positive note, it will not take as long to reprogram as it did to get into this habit in the first place.

Dr. B. Timothy Walsh, and his team at Columbia Center for Eating Disorders, use the habit model to treat disordered eating and eating disorders. He states that the current thinking is that habits are not forgotten, even if they have not been engaged in for a long time. It makes sense that behaviors become habitual when they are rewarding and are done multiple times.[2] For example, having a bowl of ice cream instead of doing your homework right after you get off the bus after school every day. The key is to substitute the old habit with a new one. In other words, don't just grit your teeth when feeling a pull toward the ice cream without hunger. When you have the first inkling, let's say you are taking your first step toward the refrigerator, that is when you engage in a new habit (ultimately it would be the same new behavior every single time so that it can become the new automatic behavior), like squeezing a stress ball, taking a walk around the block, or art-making. The challenge is to develop a new habitual behavior that is rewarding as well. Squeezing a stress ball doesn't compare to a bowl of ice cream, so you've got to find a way to "fun up" your new habit. So, maybe eating an apple and watching 30 minutes of TV would work better.

This way you are creating a new groove, not just withering away the old one. Whipping out some pastels and paper in response to the cue of walking toward the fridge will become the new automatic behavior in response to the cue. Heck, wallpapering your walls with all your new art could be rewarding, at least until your mom gets home.

Dr. Walsh goes on to say that a new repetitive behavior is like a hula-hoop in your brain. The more you engage in a behavior, the stronger is the feedback loop that goes from your prefrontal cortex (thinking brain) to a deeper structure in the brain over time (also known as the dorsal striatum, if you're looking for ways to impress your friends). In other words, it's like there are loops between the prefrontal and the striatum in continuous feedback, and as they are practiced they move further back in the brain and deeper in their positioning. With practice, the same cue (urge to eat without hunger) will be paired with a new motor activity, like art-making, for example. And over time the urges will diminish all together, with occasional emotional eating, which is totally normal.

Foodless Fulfillment

Learning to regulate emotions in ways other than food is one part of the equation, finding foodless fulfillment is the other. If you have a history of trying to soothe yourself with food, you'll want to invest in foodless fulfillment. What do you love to do? Do you love yoga, tennis, drawing, gardening, or blogging? Doing things that light you up—following your greatest passions as part of your normal routine—will fill you up from the inside in a way food never could.

Foodless fulfillment will be key to keeping food in its place, and eating with a legit starting place. Doing things that inspire you is a great way to keep your mind from wandering. By following your greatest passions, you're more likely to be in the zone and present in the moment. Trying to use food for that purpose will never leave you feeling filled up from the inside.

Commit to increasing the activities in your life that "boost" you. I'm talking about those passions that place you in the flow of life and keep you closest to the natural state of your body's wisdom. When we eat food without appetite, our eating ends up preoccupying us because we are pulling the wrong tool out of the toolbox, leaving us out of alignment. Now, not all of us know what it is we are passionate about. In that case, it requires taking the time to explore a mix of activities that you feel at least somewhat propelled toward. What are you pulled to do?

Activities I Can Do When I Am Not Hungry But I Want Food

Make a list! This exercise is an opportunity to list out the things that you love to do, those things that really fill you up. When you are relaxed and focused, write down a few things that make you feel in flow. We have a sample list below. This doesn't have to be complicated or long, it just has to be about what you like. We recommend filling out 10 activities. You can always come back and edit, add, or cross off items.

The next time you feel an urge to eat without hunger, go to your list. Experiment by doing a few of the activities on the list that are possible at that time. See what happens. The goal is to pull you towards something meaningful in that moment, and away from emotional eating. Sometimes you are going to eat for reasons that are not related to appetite and that's okay. The point is that you begin to recognize those moments and, over time, make choices that are actually fulfilling for you.

- Go to my movie queue—do I feel like watching a thriller, comedy, animé?

- Head toward your "creative space" (see Habit Reversal with Art below)

- Dance

- Play a musical instrument

- Color in a coloring book

- Paint my nails

- Shave my legs

- Walk around a bookstore

- Listen to music

- Step outside for a moment and hone into a sound in nature

- Go to a local art show

Now, make your list.

ACTIVITIES I CAN DO WHEN I AM NOT HUNGRY BUT I WANT FOOD

1. _____
   _____

2. _____
   _____

3. _____
   _____

4. _____
   _____

5. _____
   _____

6. _____
   _____

7. _____
   _____

8. _____
   _____

9. _____
   _____

10. _____
    _____

Habit Reversal with Art: Redesign Your Relationship with Food

Margaret Hunter, an art therapist who writes about the importance of availability and abundance of art materials says: "The table with art supplies becomes a metaphor for the table set with food, both providing a kind of nourishment." When you feel a pull toward food without hunger, Margaret asserts, art-making is something you can engage in to get your creative juices flowing. Recurring engagement with art materials provides opportunities for activating the five senses: sight, smell, taste, touch, and sound. New experiences that stimulate the brain enhance potential for growth, habit reversal, and a new kind of foodless fulfillment.[3]

To increase the likeliness of making art, the best possible environment for creativity should be established. Begin by designating a table or area that you can call your creative space. Select a variety of art materials and place them so they are visible and easily accessible. Place a protective covering on your table or space so you can feel free to be as creative as you want to be! Once you have established your creative space you can play with the art materials any way you like.

Some useful, fun art materials:

- papers in different sizes and colors

- scissors, glue, and tape

- hole punch

- fabric and ribbon scraps

- coloring books

- pencils, pencil sharpener, and eraser

- markers, pastels paints, and brushes

- buttons, discarded jewelry, and shiny objects

- feathers

- modeling clay

- whatever else you can think of!

Train of Thought

Think of the next exercise as a train that has a specific destination—in this case the destination is connected eating. But sometimes it gets derailed, lost, and occasionally hijacked. As you can see from the example below, one sequence leads from one behavior to another, ultimately a railroad that leads to certain foodie behaviors. If you can become skilled at knowing what triggers lead to your derailment, you will develop the insight you need to change behaviors.

Use the client sample below to get a feel for how this intervention works. Do your best to describe each blank section with as much excruciating detail as you can—don't be shy!

Internal/external stressors: I got less than 6 hours of sleep last night.

Prompting event: When I logged into Instagram I saw multiple pictures of my friends out doing fun things together that I didn't get invited to.

Thoughts and feelings: I noticed thoughts about no one liking me, and I had a feeling of loneliness.

Problem behavior: Eating a bunch of food without hunger.

Consequences: Worried that I gained weight. Also feel physically uncomfortable because I ate too much.

Target behavior (the behavior that if addressed would create the most amount of change): The feelings were recall, not reality—I remember telling my friends I couldn't do anything because I had too much homework to go out. I also need to get myself off to bed in time to get an adequate night's sleep. I notice my brain is particularly attracted to bad news when I'm sleep deprived.

TRAIN OF THOUGHT

Internal/external stressors: _____

_____

_____

_____

Prompting event: _____

_____

_____

_____

Thoughts and feelings: _____

_____

_____

_____

Problem behavior: _____

_____

_____

_____

Consequences: _____

_____

_____

_____

Target behavior: _____

_____

_____

_____

_____

Creating Space Between You and Non-Hunger Eating

Commit to creating space between you and non-hunger eating by writing about what is going on with you that has nothing to do with food. This next exercise will help you strengthen your ability to delay gratification so that you can make it over the hump. Don't be discouraged if at first what you end up doing with food stays the same. If you persist, the delay will have a ripple effect on your food intake over time. Name where you are on the Hunger Meter, and any thoughts that you notice.

> *Where I am on the Hunger Meter*: I'm at about a "6" on the Hunger Meter because I had a hearty lunch about 30 minutes ago.
>
> *Thoughts I noticed*: "The chocolate-covered caramels in the fridge sound good right now." I think I'm feeling a pull toward the candy because I just need a break from studying.

CREATING SPACE BETWEEN YOU AND NON-HUNGER EATING

Where I am on the Hunger meter: _____

_____

_____

_____

_____

_____

_____

_____

_____

_____

_____

_____

Thoughts I noticed: _____

_____

_____

_____

_____

_____

_____

_____

_____

_____

_____

_____

_____

Chapter 12

Food and Body Image for Special Events

Unless you're from the planet Mars, your pursuit for thinness will increase when you have an event coming up for which you want to look good. Let's take as an example the "Spring Fling." As if seeing your teachers at night wasn't unexpectedly awkward enough, we start hamster-wheeling about how we're going to lose weight for the big day. It's not uncommon for people to not even go to their events because of their weight. It's time to swap your strategy and understand the real story about attractiveness.

It is well documented that we are all attracted to happy people, those that are not internally sucked into their own misery. So, yeah, physicality might come into play in that first 5–10 minutes of seeing someone, but, beyond that, we are like bees to honey for happy people. Keep in mind it's ultimately the negative thoughts about your body that are throwing you off your game, not your actual body.

Worry-thoughts, whether they are about not being thin enough, chiseled enough...emit insecurity, and insecurity is unappealing in any color. Body dissatisfaction takes us away from our happiness, which is a problem if you are aiming for attractiveness, given that happy is the new hot.

Two Extreme Behaviors When Trying to Look Good for an Upcoming Event

First, there is the infamous and wildly self-defeating Weight Loss Effort Before the Event. This plan, executed on sheer willpower alone, is like holding your breath; and we all know what happens after you hold your breath too long. Remember, when restricting your food, you are ultimately eating below your metabolic rate, basically hanging out in a semi-starvation state.

Note to self: your body doesn't care about whatever fancy-pants event you have coming up. It doesn't know you are trying to look cool; it is only concerned with keeping you alive. (I know; big deal, right?) So, while some measure of quick weight loss may take place (probably water weight), it can cost you your presence and promote a sluggish metabolism, not to mention that it also makes you no fun to be with. Many of you will have heard the term "hangry"—hungry + angry = hangry. When your hunger comes on with a vengeance, and believe us, it will, you will no longer be running your food, it will start running you.

Your obsession with food can overtake you to the point where you end up missing the event in real time. So, while everyone is lining up to dance with the happy hot person, you'll be the wallflower obsessing about ice cream.

The second outdated, weight-obsessed maneuver is the plan to restrict your food intake at the actual event. Your fear of a protruding belly (c'mon, don't deny it) may drive you to swear an oath to fill up on only healthy food in an attempt not to eat what you perceive to be the "fattening" food awaiting you. Whether it's your pursuit of a flat stomach or your pursuit of a six pack, it may drive you to an even more unreasonable oath in which you promise not to eat anything at the event at all. Both are hollow plans that should get checked at the door with our coat.

Let's rework the plan. If happy is the new hot, then why not intentionally focus on thoughts that give you more access to your inner state of happiness? Which thought feels better?

1. "I'm gonna rock this party."

2. "OMG, I don't look like____ (whoever you think is smokin' hot), so I'm nothing."

Your goal should be to imagine how you do want the event to go. How do you want to feel about the people there? How do you want people to feel about you? Mantra idea: "I draw in people who like me just as I am."

Spend time thinking about how you are going to eat with body awareness before the event: with authentic appetite, honoring cravings, and stopping at just enough. As for eating at the event itself, you might even be excited to have access to fun foods you don't normally have. Envision yourself arriving near a Level 3 on the Hunger Meter so you can get a good read on what you'd truly like to eat once you're there. Most importantly, imagine exuding confidence at the event; knowing who you are.

Following this direction will lead you peacefully down the path of body positivity for an event, eating out at a restaurant, or holiday eating. And remember, better-feeling thoughts cancel out the dysregulated emotion that typically pulls us toward food without hunger.

How You See Others Is How They See You[1]

There are multiple things people look for and consider when we find someone attractive: a good listener, someone who treats their friends well, happy, friendly, style, security, people who see our goodness. Explore this in the next exercise. See our sample below, using actor Jennifer Lawrence, to generate ideas for your own answers and add those in the blank space provided on the next page.

Think of someone you find attractive: Jennifer Lawrence

What are 7 things you find attractive about this person?

1. She's not like a typical celebrity, she's herself (authentic).

2. She doesn't seem to conform to what most celebrities do.

3. Famous for speaking out about her body and refusing to lose weight for roles.

4. Not afraid to laugh at herself; when she tripped at the Grammys she laughed it off.

5. She's really talented at her craft.

6. She knows who she is, and comfortable in her own skin.

7. She's not afraid to stand up against inequitable pay for fear of being liked less.

HOW YOU SEE OTHERS IS HOW THEY SEE YOU

Think of someone you find attractive:

_____

What are 7 things you find attractive about this person?

1. _____

   _____

2. _____

   _____

3. _____

   _____

4. _____

   _____

5. _____

   _____

6. _____

   _____

7. _____

   _____

Old Story/New Story

Special events are great occasions for rewriting negative stories and replacing them with new ones. Here's an example from one our clients of her old story, the new story she developed for herself, and the steps she took to get there:

"Old" Story

All the other kids at the dance are going to be skinnier than me. You only get one chance at an event like this, and if I'm fat it will ruin my memories of the night. The worst part is that my body will be memorialized in the pictures people decide to post on social media without my permission.

"New" Story

I like knowing that the more I envision myself feeling uniquely beautiful at the event, the better my chances are of actually feeling that way in real time. I can think of many things that I can appreciate about my own beauty as well as the beauty of others. I may not have total body acceptance at this time, but no one is scrutinizing the way I look like I am. Good-feeling thoughts emit positivity, and that is what people will be noticing about me. Besides, thoughts are just content, not reality.

Action Taken to Support My New Story

I will spend 3 minutes each morning for the days before the event thinking or writing about how I do want to feel about myself when I'm there. I will repeat the mantra, "I look plenty good enough."

OLD STORY/NEW STORY

"Old" Story

_____
_____
_____
_____
_____
_____
_____
_____
_____
_____
_____

"New" Story

_____
_____
_____
_____
_____
_____
_____
_____
_____
_____
_____

Action Taken to Support My New Story

_____

_____

_____

_____

_____

_____

_____

_____

_____

_____

_____

_____

Journal Meets Vision Board: Set Your Intent for the Event

Journaling accesses both the right- and left-brain hemispheres reducing emotionally aroused states, while vision boarding utilizes magazine cutouts to bring what you are journaling to life. Journaling and vision boards are like a combo meal, the sauce to your nuggets, they go together. Leaf through magazines and cut out any images that you feel drawn to related to your upcoming event. For example, you might see an image of a peace sign, cut it out and glue it in your journal, and write the words around the image, "I breathe in peace about my upcoming event, and I breathe out anxiety."

You will need a journal, glue stick, magazine cutouts, and scissors. Make your vision board on the blank space provided on the next page or use your own personal journal. Consider the following:

- How do I want to feel about other people at the event?

- How do I want other people to feel about me when I'm there?

- What positive thoughts will I commit to about the food and eating at the event?

- What positive thoughts will I devote to thinking about my overall appearance as well as the goodness in me?

JOURNAL MEETS VISION BOARD:
SET YOUR INTENT FOR THE EVENT

Cope Ahead for an Event

Practice ahead of time increases the chances of performing a desired skill or behavior. In this example below, you'll see a list of food-related triggers a client often had at restaurants, and her list of new emotional responses to practice. Think of an event (large or small) that you're planning to attend. First, write down all of the potential "triggers" you think you might experience at the event (they lose some of their potency when you identify them). Then, list some new and/or alternative emotional responses. It works best if you write out this skill a few days ahead then practice "imaginally" as the event draws nearer.

Potential Triggers	New Emotional Responses
The portions served at the restaurant I'm going to are huge!	I will remind myself that there's more where that came from, I can stop at just enough, take the rest home, and eat it again when I'm hungry...it's not my last chance!
I usually order what I think I should order, not what I actually want.	I will commit to ordering exactly what I'm craving versus making my selection based on fat/calorie content. I am aware that satisfaction is both getting the food you want as well as stopping at a comfortable place.
Talking to other people distracts me, making it difficult to stop at just enough.	I will arrive near a "3" on the Hunger Meter so it's easier for me to gauge when I'm done. I will remind myself that the waiter/waitress has no idea where I am on the Hunger Meter, it's up to me to decide when I've had enough.
My food during the week is so "healthy" and lacking pleasure, that I overly respond to tasty food.	I will make sure I include pleasure in my food selections during the week so I don't overly respond to satisfying food.

COPE AHEAD FOR AN EVENT

Potential Triggers	New Emotional Responses
_____	_____
_____	_____
_____	_____
_____	_____
_____	_____
_____	_____
_____	_____

Chapter 13

The More Often You Weigh, the More You'll Weigh

Scales Are for Fake Snakes

Have you heard the old story about the kid who is camping with his family and walks into their cabin, sees a snake in the corner and runs out full blast with hands waving in the air, screaming? Usually, Mom or Dad, hearing the screams and seeing their kid run like a mad person down the tree lane decide to check it out. They slowly walk up to the cabin, push the creaky door open with a stick, step carefully into the room after peering around the side of the door, and quickly flip on the light. Ready to scream themselves, they stop, mouth half open. What do they see?

That's right, they see a horrifying, snarled, thick, winding... rope lying in the corner. Suddenly, all the fear that was there goes away and usually everyone laughs after they're done being mad at being so scared. This example helps people conquer fears about what they perceive as opposed to what's really there. How does this apply to a scale? Well, a scale is the fake snake. Sometimes, a scale gives us the information that we think is true, and not what's real. Confusing? Well, let us explain.

Most of us have an exaggerated startle response to our scale. Our fear of it is greater than what it can actually record.

Much like our fear of snakes, our brain records anything negative in nature to help us learn from our history. Psychologist
Rick Hanson says, "We've got a brain that is like Velcro for
bad experiences but Teflon for good ones." The ability to avoid
harm is key to our survival, but activating your negativity bias
as it relates to your bathroom scale, does not exactly help you
get the most out of your brain.[1]

We have this idea about what we think our weight should
be and that generally has nothing to do with where our body
actually wants to be. That idea is "learned," not innate. You
might be conditioned to think you'd only see a snake inside
a camping cabin and not, let's say, at your favorite clothing
store in the mall.

In a culture that tells all of us we should be living in a
smaller body if we are female, a more chiseled body if we are
male, or just plain better body, regardless of whether or not
we identify with a gender at all, we start to believe there is a
"right way" to be. For some a lower weight is a natural weight
for them and for others a higher weight is more natural for
them. Point being, all of these things are ideas and perceptions
and not the truth. It, too, is the fake snake.

When we weigh more on a given day, even if it is a little, we
are inclined to cut down what, and how much, we are eating.
When we "diet," our body doesn't know if this is a choice or
if there just isn't enough food available. Being "up" a bit on
the scale tends to cause us to panic and restrict our food,
immediately cutting ourselves off from our body's signals.
That's a threat to survival.

So, the body, being smart and survival oriented, wants to
be safe again. It achieves safety by trying to get you to eat.
This chemical drive to be safe and get food into the body
can lead someone who is just not eating enough, and feeling
hungry, to overeat. In the end, we can end up feeling like we
did something wrong by eating, when in reality what we did is

let ourselves get scared by the scale in the first place. When we react out of fear the problem rarely gets fixed. Unfortunately, that's what scales do, they promote reactivity and can scare us, and we end up running away from the snake and sometimes make decisions that can hurt our bodies. The fake snake keeps us worried about minor fluctuations in weight (when, really, it's just a rope).

In reality, teenagers have to grow taller and their muscles have to get larger and stronger and the bones that support their frame have to grow in length and density. Even if you know you're not growing taller anymore, some weight gain is actually still expected into your teen and young adult years. Our bodies are a dynamic system and the teen years are filled with change that is related to hormone changes and a great deal of development that is yet to happen.

One way to think of it is that you are building the house that you are going to live in. And every house is different. The house may look fashionable on the outside but, if the foundation isn't strong, it's going to have many more problems over time compared to a house that is well built and taken care of.

The path to long-term food and body contentment, your "happily ever after," the cherry on top to this whole process, is the freedom to throw away the scale. There's nothing like a battery-operated device to pull you right out of your natural state. Weighing yourself regularly promotes scrutiny, and scrutiny breeds dissatisfaction—which is way opposite of a loving feeling.

If the number on the scale happens to be a bit lower, then we can feel good. But the interesting question here is, what part of us feels good? It's the ego—the part of us that's chronically dissatisfied. Bottom line, the kind of overeating or undereating that occurs by closely monitoring our weight on a scale overrules our ability to eat in response to our body's wisdom. Our preoccupation keeps us out of the present moment. Worrying about the future or freaking out about the past leads to an imbalanced self. And what do we do when we're imbalanced? We eat—without true hunger. Hence, the more often you weigh, the more you'll weigh.

And what does that number mean anyway? Scales are incredibly inaccurate. For one, you can check your weight on four different scales and get four different results. Or, you can go to bed and weigh a few pounds lighter than when you wake up the next morning. How is that possible? It's not! Scales often reflect fluid status in the body (are you hydrated or dehydrated?), and can shift depending on whether you have eaten, how much fluid you have consumed, whether you are premenstrual, or whether you have used the bathroom or not.

Avid weight checkers may check their weight in the morning, in the afternoon, and at night. Those people can tell you that their weight fluctuates throughout the day. They are often stressed out, and can't explain how they have gained and lost so much weight in one day. Often these individuals express distress that their weight is "all over the place." However, that's just not the case and it's more a matter of perception and overdoing it with the scale.

That's why we recommend getting rid of your scale entirely. Throw it in the trash or remove the batteries and bury it in your backyard. Ignorance—in this case, of the number on the scale which can be all over the place—really is bliss! Replace weighing yourself with an investment in developing a more positive attitude about your body. Eventually, this positive attitude will become your new and vastly improved companion. By recognizing the false messages related to health and empowering ourselves with accurate and positive information, while also becoming experts at meeting our needs, we can battle the fake snakes.

You've probably noticed that if 10 things happen in a day and one was bad (like your weight being "up" on the scale), and nine were good, it's the one negative thing that will take precedence in the brain. It takes *way* more of a positive thought to cancel out a negative one.

Replacing body dissatisfaction with a ritual of taking in the good, the next exercise highlights the work of neuro-psychologist Rick Hanson. Over time you can slowly reshape the brain and increase the plasticity for positivity in the brain (bonus: this part of the brain will get more and more buffed every time you practice this).

Small Bites of Positivity

1. *Think about something good that has happened today* (it does not need to be a million-dollar moment): The coziness of the baggy black turtleneck sweater I'm wearing today. I thank it for being the coziest thing ever, yet also being quite stylish. I can pass for wearing a cute outfit while wearing heaven. The simplest things can bring the most joy, and I have to say, when I'm in a baggy black turtleneck sweater, I'm in a pleasant mood.

2. *Mull over that good thing for about 10 to 30 seconds*: I thought about it for 20 seconds at a time throughout the day at school.

3. *Repeat 5, 10, 20 times a day:* I did this five times during the day; the last time was right before going to bed.

SMALL BITES OF POSITIVITY

1. Think about something good that has happened today (it does not need to be a million-dollar moment):

   _____

   _____

   _____

   _____

   _____

   _____

   _____

   _____

2. Mull over that good thing for about 10 to 30 seconds:

   _____

   _____

   _____

   _____

   _____

   _____

   _____

3. Repeat 5, 10, 20 times a day:

   _____

   _____

   _____

   _____

   _____

   _____

Goodbye Letter to My Scale

Writing a goodbye letter to your scale will make you aware of how it served you, so you can replace that maladaptive coping mechanism with one that has a more prolonged state of well-being. Below is an example of a letter written by a client. Please use the blank lines on the next page to write your own goodbye letter.

How was my scale's job?

My scale was part of my morning ritual. I cannot tell you how thankful I am for its presence, just seeing it when I walked into the bathroom each morning, gave me certainty. It let me know where I stand, gave me something to strive for, a goal, a purpose. It gave me a preoccupation, which to be honest, was sometimes easier to focus on than what I was really upset about. It told me how to feel that day. If the number was down, I felt elated, if the number was "up," I felt anxious.

Am I ready to put my scale out of a job?

Though the scale was my morning companion. I no longer need it. I am ready to shift my gaze, and focus on the things in life that give me a sense of purpose. Focusing on a minor fluctuation in my weight takes me away from my true values. I am ready to lay down the control model I've been using with my body image and food, and make a shift into the trust model with connected eating. I have learned that weighing myself has kept me making food decisions from the "chin up" and I am now ready to trust the intelligence of my body. I am ready for my weight to land wherever it wants to so I can show up in a way that matches who I really am. I now know that I cannot strive to be a weight lower than where my body wants to be and do what I was meant to do in this life.

GOODBYE LETTER TO MY SCALE

_____

_____

_____

_____

_____

_____

_____

_____

_____

_____

_____

_____

_____

_____

_____

_____

_____

_____

_____

_____

_____

_____

_____

_____

_____

_____

A plan of action is like the GPS feature on your smartphone. It starts by identifying the current obstacles getting in the way of where you'd like to go (like a traffic jam, or roadwork). The goals are about where you'd like to go or your end in view (an example would be accepting your body's natural weight). Of course, we also need the measurements, which are the observable ways you will know you are headed in the right direction (like landmarks).

Plan of Action

Choose a personal issue you care about, and create a plan of action. Identify the problem, come up with goals, and decide how you'll measure your progress. Choose an issue that is important for you, and think about what feels off or like you are not moving in the right direction. Identify where you are with it, where you want to go, and how you are going to track your progress. By having a map, you can see if you are staying on path and remember your starting and end point.

Plan of action for: Accepting my body as it is today.

Identify problems (negative thoughts, behaviors, or feelings that are holding you back):

1. Weighing myself on a scale has made it impossible to stay on track with connected eating because it takes me away from my body's innate wisdom.

2. Comparing my body to someone else's body on social media.

3. Adhering to the culture's narrow definition of beauty.

Goals (big picture ways you would like to be different):

1. To be a fearless eater.

2. To have less preoccupation with my weight and shape, more focus on my purpose in life.

3. To change how I see, not how I look.

Observable measurements (to help you know you are achieving your goals):

1. When I look in the mirror I dislike my body less.

2. I notice I am doing a daily practice of taking in the good, and it's becoming easier.

3. I have less anxiety about where my body weight is going to land, it appears to be stable, based on my clothes fitting.

PLAN OF ACTION

Plan of action for:

_____

_____

_____

_____

Identify problems (negative thoughts, behaviors, or feelings that are holding you back):

_____

_____

_____

_____

_____

Goals (big picture ways you would like to be different):

_____

_____

_____

_____

_____

Observable measurements (to help you know you are achieving your goals):

_____

_____

_____

_____

_____

Write Out the Fantasy of Being "Thin"—All the Way

"Destination addiction" is a term used to describe a pre-occupation with the idea that happiness is in the next place.[2] Losing weight is a common example of this. "If only I weighed less, then I would be happy." Fantasy, in and of itself, is neutral. Fantasy can be nourishing or it can be unhealthy. When we fantasize about being smaller than where our body naturally wants to be, we are taking up emotional real estate that could be used for thoughts that are life affirming. We typically think about only the perceived good aspects of our fantasy.

Jill's story is about her fantasy of being thin. Take a look and think about this idea of "destination addiction," and the idea that happiness lies elsewhere. How does this relate to you and the issue with which you might also have "destination addiction"? Are you waiting to be happy?

JILL'S FANTASY OF BEING THIN: 15 YEARS OLD

When I was first asked to do this assignment of writing out what the reality of the fantasy of being "thin" would be, including the good and the bad, I felt a bit confused. Honestly, what would be bad about being thin? I hadn't even thought about it before. My fantasy-land is so deeply entrenched with the "good" that there wasn't room left in my mind for any potential drawbacks. Now that I've considered it, I can think of a few pretty big ones.

First, here are the good things I have told myself I would experience if I were "thin" (which is not my natural weight):

I wouldn't be the "fat" sister anymore. I've built so much of my personal identity around my size compared to my sisters. It would be so awesome to not be the "fat" one anymore. I can easily visualize how amazing it would feel to be the same size as them and the confidence it would give me. Shopping would be awesome! I'd zip in and out of stores and scoop up all the things I really want to wear, but don't think I can pull off. I wouldn't be worried about whether things come in my size or whether people will stare at me for my size if I try to wear something a little weird. Crop tops here I come!

What would be wrong:

Those good things would feel awesome, but unless I'm able to ingest some magical pill for living in a smaller body, being thin requires some pretty big sacrifices, since it is not my body's natural size.

This would come with a lot of rules around eating. If I were thin, it would require me being restrictive with my food. I know firsthand how terrible it is to deprive yourself when you're on a diet. I imagine that even if I lost weight to get to a weight that was not natural for me, I would have to be very controlled around food for the rest of my life. So, instead of having external people judging me for my choices, my inner critic would be loud and proud forever. It would rob me of a peaceful relationship with food.

I imagine I would be forced into punishing exercise. I like walking and the occasional yoga or hip-hop dance class. I don't think these would be enough to keep me "thin," so much more of my day and life would be dedicated to not-so-enjoyable-for-me exercise. It would impair my relationship to balanced exercise.

Lastly, I would be agreeing to the culture's narrow definition of beauty instead of expanding it. I am in charge of my agreements, and I choose to change the way I see, not the way I look.

WRITE OUT THE FANTASY OF BEING "THIN"—ALL THE WAY

_____

_____

_____

_____

_____

_____

_____

_____

_____

_____

_____

_____

_____

_____

_____

_____

_____

_____

_____

_____

_____

_____

_____

_____

_____

Conclusion

The teen years are a fantastic time of growth, change, and development. By understanding that this change is universal to all as well as unique to you, we hope that you have gained insight into your own needs. Our goal continues to be to provide you with tools that give you more knowledge and a broader view of nutrition and well-being. Always go back to the basics, make time for yourself. Eat and enjoy everything with a strong foundation of balance. Make choices that work for you and that have also been shown to be scientifically critical, such as having a regulated sleep schedule, turning off the tech, and letting your mind power down. Be mindful and willing to take a moment to really feel your feelings, hone in on hunger cues or emotional cues, and identify what the true need is in that moment (coffee to mask fatigue or a nap to allow rest). Step into the solution (I'm taking a nap, creating a pros and cons list, talking to a trusted person in my life) and then move on.

We get good at what we do most often. So, practice eating, working, exercising, and taking care of yourself with joy. Build inner wisdom through these tools, and make choices from a place that is reinforced with a positive relationship with food and your environment. Be well...

Resources

Jennifer J. Thomas, Ph.D. and Jenni Schaefer, *Almost Anorexic: Is My (or My Loved One's) Relationship with Food a Problem?* **Center City: Hazelden (2013).**
Determine if you (or your loved one's) relationship with food is a problem, gain insight on how to intervene with a loved one and discover scientifically proven strategies to change unhealthy eating patterns. Also, learn when and how to get professional help when it's needed.

Use this link to get automatic results from the Compulsive Exercise Test (CET): www.jennischaefer.com/cet.

New Moon Girls
Girl-created media since 1993. In New Moon Girls' award-winning magazine and online community (www.newmoon.com), girls use emotional support, self-expression, and healthy resistance to stay deeply connected to their true interests, abilities, and hopes.

National Eating Disorders Association
NEDA supports individuals and families affected by eating disorders, and serves as a catalyst for prevention, cures, and access to quality care. Worried that you or someone you care about is struggling with an eating disorder? Early detection and intervention is key to recovery. Take the

National Eating Disorders Association's free and confidential screening today to learn if it is time to seek professional help: www.nationaleatingdisorders.org/screening-tool.

For treatment options, visit www.nationaleatingdisorders. org or contact NEDA's Live Helpline: 1.800.931.2237.

The Body Positive

Teens and young adults learn how to create Body Positive programs on their campuses to help their peers have positive self-image, balanced eating and exercise habits, and experience their unique beauty. Since 1996, The Body Positive (www.thebodypositive.org) has been helping students create peer-led programs to prevent eating disorders and provide students who are suffering over their bodies a safe place to share their concerns. Contact: info@thebodypositive.org or 510.528.0101.

Well Now

Well Now (www.lucyaphramor.com) teaches body respect and health-gain for all. It is a compassion-centered approach to helping people understand their eating and make peace with food and their bodies. As part of this exploration it considers the bigger picture of health and pays attention to trauma. Thus, it links self-care and social justice. Email: lucy.aphramor@gmail.com.

Recommended Reading on Sleep

Ken Berger, "In multibillion-dollar business of NBA, sleep is the biggest debt." *CBS Sports*, June 7 (2016). Accessed on 02/14/2018 at www.cbssports.com/nba/news/in-multi-billion-dollar-business-of-nba-sleep-is-the-biggest-debt.

Daniel Gallan, "Sleeping on the job: the importance of rest for peak performance." *CONQA Group*, August 6, 2015. Accessed on 02/14/2018 at www.conqasport.com/sleep-performance-recovery.

Arianna Huffington, *The Sleep Revolution: Transforming Your Life, One Night at a Time.* New York: Harmony Crown (2017).

James Maas, *Power Sleep: The Revolutionary Program That Prepares Your Mind for Peak Performance.* New York: Quill/HarperCollins (1999).

James Maas, Davis, Hayley A., and Robbins, Rebecca, *Sleep to Win!: Secrets to Unlocking Your Athletic Excellence in Every Sport.* Bloomington, IN: Author House (2013).

James Maas, Robbins, Rebecca S., Driscoll, Sharon R., Appelbaum, Hannah R., and Platt, Samantha L., *Sleep for Success: Everything You Must Know about Sleep But Are Too Tired to Ask.* Bloomington, IN: Author House (2011).

Jenny Vrentas, "Lights out football." *Sports Illustrated*, November 11, 2015. Accessed on 02/14/2018 at http://mmqb.si.com/mmqb/2015/11/11/how-the-science-of-sleep-is-transforming-the-nfl#.

References

Chapter 1

1. Anita Johnston, National Eating Disorder Week event, State Theatre, Modesto, CA, March 2, 2017.
2. Amanda McCorquodale, "8 'fake it 'til you make it' strategies backed by science." *Mental Floss*, February 2, 2016. Accessed on 02/08/2018 at http://mentalfloss.com/article/74310/8-fake-it-til-you-make-it-strategies-backed-science.
3. Stephanie Burg, "7 things women who love their bodies do each day." *Mind Body Green*, June 23, 2015. Accessed on 02/08/2018 at www.mindbodygreen.com/0-20409/7-things-women-who-love-their-bodies-do-each-day.html.

Chapter 2

1. Bruce Simons-Mortona, Neil Lerner, and Jeremiah Singer, "The observed effects of teenage passengers on the risky driving behavior of teenage drivers." *Accident Analysis & Prevention 37*(6) (2005): 973–982. Jason Chein, Dustin Albert, Lia O'Brien, Kaitlyn Uckert, and Laurence Steinberg, "Peers increase adolescent risk taking by enhancing activity in the brain's reward circuitry." *Developmental Science 14*(2) (2011), F1–F10.
2. Signe Darpinian, phone interview with Dr. Louann Brizendine, February 23, 2017.
3. Donald L. Fisher, Jeff Caird, William Horrey, and Lana Trick, *Handbook of Teen and Novice Drivers: Research, Practice, Policy, and Directions*. New York: CRC Press (2016).

Chapter 4

1. Allison Aubrey, "Sleep munchies: why it's harder to resist snacks when we're tired." *All Things Considered, NPR*, March 2, 2016. Accessed on 02/12/2018 at www.npr.org/sections/thesalt/2016/03/02/468933610/sleep-munchies-why-its-harder-to-resist-snacks-when-were-tired.
2. Karen Koenig, *The Rules of "Normal" Eating: A Commonsense Approach for Dieters, Overeaters, Undereaters, Emotional Eaters, and Everyone in Between!* Carlsbad, CA: Gurze Books (2005), p.29.
3. In James B. Maas, *Power Sleep: The Revolutionary Program That Prepares Your Mind for Peak Performance*. New York: Perennial Currents (1999), p.15.
4. Kyle Hill, "The physics of Fred Flintstone's flaming feet." *Scientific American*, April 22, 2013. Accessed on 02/12/2018 at https://blogs.scientificamerican.com/guest-blog/the-physics-of-fred-flintstones-flaming-feet.
5. Aric A. Prather, Denise Janicki-Deverts, Martica H. Hall, and Sheldon Cohen, "Behaviorally assessed sleep and susceptibility to the common cold." *Sleep: Journal of Sleep Research & Sleep Medicine 38*(9) (2015): 1353–1359. Accessed on 02/12/2018 at https://doi.org/10.5665/sleep.4968.

6.   Vicky Rideout, *The Common Sense Census: Media Use by Tweens and Teens*. San Francisco: Common Sense Media (2015). Accessed on 02/12/2018 at www.commonsensemedia.org/sites/default/files/uploads/research/census_executivesummary.pdf.
7.   Lindsey Tanner, "Caffeine consumption, mainly from soda, common in kids and teens." *Associated Press*, February 10, 2014. Accessed on 02/12/2018 at www.nydailynews.com/life-style/health/kids-teens-regular-caffeine-buzz-study-article-1.1608612. Diane C. Mitchell, Carol A. Knight, Jon Hockenberry, Robyn Teplansky, and Terryl J. Hartman, "Beverage caffeine intakes in the U.S." *Food and Chemical Toxicology 63* (2014): 136–142. Accessed on 02/12/2018 at https://doi.org/10.1016/j.fct.2013.10.042.
8.   James B. Mass, et al. *Sleep for Success! Everything You Must Know about Sleep but Are Too Tired to Ask*. AuthorHouse (2011), pp.58–88.

Chapter 5
1.   Vaughn W. Barry, Meghan Baruth, Michael W. Beets, J. Larry Durstine, Jihong Liu, and Steven N. Blair, "Fitness vs. fatness on all-cause mortality: a meta-analysis." *Progress in Cardiovascular Diseases 56*(4) (2014): 382–390.
2.   Connie Sobczak, *Embody: Learning to Love Your Unique Body (and Quiet That Critical Voice!)*. Carlsbad, CA: Gurze Books (2014), p.114.
3.   Deborah R. Glasofer and Joanna Steinglass, "Disrupting the habits of anorexia: how a patient learned to escape the rigid routines of an eating disorder." *Scientific American*, September 1, 2016. Accessed on 02/12/2018 at www.scientificamerican.com/article/disrupting-the-habits-of-anorexia.

Chapter 9
1.   © Lucy Aphramor. Adapted and used with permission.
2.   © Lucy Aphramor. Adapted and used with permission.
3.   Jennifer Rollin, "Nutrition experts explain why you shouldn't quit sugar," *Huffington Post*, September 26, 2016. Accessed on 02/13/2018 at www.huffingtonpost.com/entry/nutrition-experts-explain-why-you-shouldnt-quit-sugar_us_57e8fbb7e4b00267764fc828.
4.   L. L. Birch, et al., "What Kind of Exposure Reduces Children's Food Neophobia?" *Appetite 9*(3) (1987): 171–178, doi:10.1016/s0195-6663(87)80011-9

Chapter 10
1.   Anita A. Johnston, *Eating in the Light of the Moon: How Women Can Transform Their Relationship with Food Through Myths, Metaphors, and Storytelling*. Carlsbad, CA: Gurze Books (2000), pp.157–158. Reproduced with permission from Gurze.

Chapter 11
1.   Jill Bolt Taylor, *My Stroke of Insight: A Brain Scientist's Personal Journey*. New York: Penguin (2009).
2.   Signe Darpinian, interview and correspondence with Dr. Timothy Walsh, April 13, 2017. For more, see http://profiles.columbiapsychiatry.org/profile/bwalsh (accessed 02/13/2018).
3.   Margaret R. Hunter, "Art Therapy and Eating Disorders." In Marcia L. Rosal and David E. Gussak (eds), *The Wiley Handbook of Art Therapy*. Hoboken, NJ: Wiley Blackwell (2016), pp.387–396.

Chapter 12
1.   Signe Darpinian, interview and correspondence with Dr. Rick Hanson, April 6, 2017.

Chapter 13
1.   Signe Darpinian, interview and correspondence with Dr. Rick Hanson, April 6, 2017.
2.   Robert Holden, *Authentic Success: Essential Lessons and Practices from the World's Leading Coaching Program on Success Intelligence*. New York: Hay House (2011), pp.251–264.